HIGH SCHOOL

—Updated!

50
CREATIVE DISCUSSIONS FOR
HIGH SCHOOL YOUTH GROUPS

DAVID LYNN

ZONDERVAN™

GRAND RAPIDS, MICHIGAN 49530

High School TalkSheets—Updated! 50 creative discussions for high school youth groups

Copyright © 2001 by Youth Specialties

Youth Specialties books, 300 S. Pierce St., El Cajon, CA 92020, are published by Zondervan, 5300 Patterson Ave. S.E., Grand Rapids, MI 49530.

Library of Congress Cataloging-in-Publication Data

Lynn, David, 1954-
    High school talksheets—updated! : 50 creative discussion starters for youth groups / David Lynn.
        p. cm.
    ISBN 0-310-23852-8
        1. Church group work with teenagers. 2. High school students—Religious life. I. Title

BV4447 .L96 2001
286'.433—dc21

00-043938

Web site addresses listed in this book were current at the time of publication, but we can't guarantee they're still operational. If you have trouble with a URL, please contact us via e-mail (YS@YouthSpecialties.com) to let us know if you've found the current or new URL or if the URL is no longer operational.

Edited by Mary Fletcher, Anita Palmer, and Tamara Rice
Interior and cover design by PAZ Design Group
Illustrations and borders by Rick Sealock

Printed in the United States of America

06 07 / VG / 15 14 13

CONTENTS

THE HOWS AND WHATS OF TALKSHEETS

You are holding a very valuable book! No, it won't make you a genius or millionaire. But it does contain 50 instant discussions for high school kids. Inside you'll find reproducible TalkSheets that cover a variety of hot topics—plus simple, step-by-step instructions on how to use them. All you need is this book, a few copies of the handouts, and some kids (and maybe a snack or two). You're on your way to landing on some serious issues in kids' lives today.

These TalkSheets are user-friendly and very flexible. They can be used in a youth group meeting, a Sunday school class, or in a Bible study group. You can adapt them for either large or small groups. And, they can be covered in only 20 minutes or explored more intensively in two hours.

You can build an entire youth group meeting around a single TalkSheet, or you can use TalkSheets to supplement other materials and resources you might be using. These are tools for you—how you use them is your choice.

High School TalkSheets—Updated! is not your average curriculum or workbook. This collection of discussions will get your kids involved and excited about talking through important issues. The TalkSheets deal with key topics and include interesting activities, challenging questions, and eye-catching graphics. They will challenge your kids to think about opinions, learn about themselves, and grow in their faith.

LEADING A TALKSHEET DISCUSSION

TalkSheets can be used as a curriculum for your youth group, but they are designed to be springboards for discussion. They encourage your kids to take part and interact with each other while talking about real life issues. And hopefully they'll do some serious thinking, discover new ideas for themselves, defend their points of view, and make decisions.

Youth today face a world of moral confusion. Youth leaders must teach the church's beliefs and values—and also help young people make the right choices in a world full of options. Teenagers are bombarded with the voices of society and the media—most of which drown out what they hear from the church.

A TalkSheet discussion works for this very reason. While dealing with the questions and activities on the TalkSheet, your kids will think carefully about issues, compare their beliefs and values with others, and make their own choices. TalkSheets will challenge your group to explain and rework their ideas in a Christian atmosphere of acceptance, support, and growth.

The most common fear of high school youth group leaders is, "What will I do if the kids in my group just sit there and don't say anything?" Well, when kids don't have anything to say, it's because they haven't had a chance or time to get their thoughts organized! Most young people haven't developed the ability to think on their feet. Since many are afraid they might sound stupid, they don't know how to voice their ideas and opinions.

The solution? TalkSheets let your kids deal with the issues in a challenging, non-threatening way before the actual discussion begins. They'll have time to organize their thoughts, write them down, and ease their fears about participating. They may even look forward to sharing their answers! Most importantly, they'll want to find out what others said and open up to talk through the topics.

If you're still a little leery about the success of a real discussion among your kids, that's okay! The only way to get them rolling is to get them started.

YOUR ROLE AS THE LEADER

The best discussions don't happen by accident. They require careful preparation and a sensitive leader. Don't worry if you aren't experienced or don't have hours to prepare. TalkSheets are designed to help even the novice leader! The more TalkSheet discussions you lead, the easier it becomes. Keep the following tips in mind when using the TalkSheets as you get your kids talking.

BE CHOOSY

Each TalkSheet deals with a different topic. Choose a TalkSheet based on the needs and the maturity level of your group. Don't feel obligated to use the TalkSheets in the order they appear in this book. Use your best judgment and mix them up however you want—they are tools for you!

MAKE COPIES

Kids will need their own copy of the TalkSheet. Only make copies of the student's side of the TalkSheet! The material on the reverse side (the leader's guide) is just for you. You're able to make copies for your group because we've given you permission to do so. U.S. copyright laws have not changed, and it is still mandatory to request permission from a publisher before making copies of other published material. It is against the law not to do so. However, permission is given for you to make copies of this material for your group only, not for every youth group in your state. Thank you for cooperating.

TRY IT YOURSELF

Once you have chosen a TalkSheet for your group, answer the questions and do the activities yourself. Imagine your kids' reactions to the TalkSheet. This will help you prepare for the discussion and understand what you are asking them to do. Plus, you'll have some time to think of other appropriate questions, activities, and Bible verses.

GET SOME INSIGHT

On each leader's guide page, you'll find numerous tips and ideas for getting the most out of your discussion. You may want to add some of your own thoughts or ideas in the margins. And, there's room to keep track of the date and the name of your group at the top of the leader's page. You'll also find suggestions for additional activities and discussion questions.

There are some references to Internet links throughout the TalkSheets. These are guides for you to find the resources and information that you need. For additional help, be sure to visit the Youth Specialties Web site at www.YouthSpecialties.com for information on materials and further links to finding what you need.

INTRODUCE THE TOPIC

It's important to introduce the topic before you pass out the TalkSheets to your group. Depending on your group, keep it short and to the point. Be careful not to over-introduce the topic, sound preachy, or resolve the issue before you've started. Your goal is to spark their interest and leave plenty of room for discussion.

The best way to do this is verbally. You can tell a story, share an experience, or describe a situation or problem having to do with the topic. You might want to jump-start your group by asking something like, "What is the first thing you think of when you hear the word _____ [insert the topic]?" Then, after a few answers have been given, you can add something like, "Well, it seems we all have different ideas about this subject. Tonight we're going to investigate it a bit further..." Then pass out the TalkSheet and be sure that everyone has a pencil or pen. Now you're on your way! The following are excellent methods you can use to introduce any topic in this book—

• Show a related short film or video.
• Read a passage from a book or magazine that relates to the subject.
• Play a popular CD that deals with the topic.
• Perform a short skit or dramatic presentation.
• Play a simulation game or role-play, setting up the topic.
• Present current statistics, survey results, or read a current newspaper article that provides recent information about the topic.
• Use an icebreaker or other crowd game, getting into the topic in a humorous way. For example if the topic is fun, play a game to begin the discussion. If the topic is success, consider a

game that helps the kids experience success or failure.

- Use posters, videos, or any other visuals to help focus attention on the topic.

There are endless possibilities for an intro—you are limited only by your own creativity! Each TalkSheet offers a few suggestions, but you are free to use any method with which you feel most comfortable. But do keep in mind that the introduction is a very important part of each session.

SET BOUNDARIES

It'll be helpful to set a few ground rules before the discussion. Keep the rules to a minimum, of course, but let the kids know what's expected of them. Here are suggestions for some basic ground rules—

- **What is said in this room stays in this room.** Emphasize the importance of confidentiality. Some kids will open up, some won't. Confidentiality is vital for a good discussion. If your kids can't keep the discussion in the room, then they won't open up.
- **No put-downs.** Mutual respect is important. If your kids disagree with some opinions, ask them to comment on the subject (but not on the other person). It's okay to attack the ideas, but not other people.
- **There is no such thing as a dumb question.** Your group members must feel free to ask questions at any time. The best way to learn is to ask questions and get answers.
- **No one is forced to talk.** Let everyone know they have the right to pass or not answer any question.
- **Only one person speaks at a time.** This is a mutual respect issue. Everyone's opinion is worthwhile and deserves to be heard.

Communicate with your group that everyone needs to respect these boundaries. If you sense that your group members are attacking each other or getting a negative attitude during the discussion, do stop and deal with the problem before going on.

ALLOW ENOUGH TIME

Pass out copies of the TalkSheet to your kids after the introduction and make sure that each person has a pen or pencil and a Bible. There are usually five or six activities on each TalkSheet. If your time is limited, or if you are using only a part of the TalkSheet, tell the group to complete only the activities you'd like them to.

Decide ahead of time whether or not you would like the kids to work on the TalkSheets individually or in groups.

Let them know how much time they have for completing the TalkSheet and let them know when there is a minute (or so) left. Go ahead and give them some extra time and then start the discussion when everyone seems ready to go.

SET THE STAGE

Create a climate of acceptance. Most teenagers are afraid to voice their opinions because they don't want to be laughed at or look stupid in front of their peers. They want to feel safe if they're going to share their feelings and beliefs. Communicate that they can share their thoughts and ideas—even if they may be different or unpopular. If your kids get put-downs, criticism, laughter, or snide comments (even if their statements are opposed to the teachings of the Bible) it'll hurt the discussion.

Always phrase your questions—even those that are printed on the TalkSheets—so that you are asking for an opinion, not an answer. For example if a question reads, "What should Bill have done in that situation?" change it to, "What do you think Bill should have done in that situation?" The simple addition of the three words "do you think" makes the question less threatening and a matter of opinion, rather than a demand for the right answer. Your kids will relax when they will feel more comfortable and confident. Plus, they'll know that you actually care about their opinions and they'll feel appreciated!

LEAD THE DISCUSSION

Discuss the TalkSheet with the group and encourage all your kids to participate. Communicate that it's important for them to respect each other's opinions and feelings! The more they contribute, the better the discussion will be.

If your youth group is big, you may divide it into smaller groups of six to 12. Each of these small groups should have a facilitator—either an adult leader or a student member—to keep the discussion going. Remind the facilitators not to dominate. If the group looks to the facilitator for an answer, ask him or her to direct the questions or responses back to the group. Once the smaller groups have completed their discussions, combine them into one large group and ask the different groups to share their ideas.

You don't have to divide the groups up with every TalkSheet. For some discussions, you may want to vary the group size and or divide the meeting into groups of the same sex.

The discussion should target the questions and answers on the TalkSheet. Go through them one at a time and ask the kids to share their responses. Have them compare their answers and brainstorm new ones in addition to the ones they've written down. Encourage them to share their opinions and answers, but don't force those who are quiet.

AFFIRM ALL RESPONSES—RIGHT OR WRONG

Let your kids know that their comments and contributions are appreciated and important. This is especially true for those who rarely speak up in group activities. Make a point of thanking them for joining in. This will be an incentive for them to participate further.

Remember that affirmation doesn't mean approval. Affirm even those comments that seem wrong to you. You'll show that everyone has a right to express their ideas—no matter how controversial they may be. If someone states an opinion that is off base, make a mental note of the comment. Then in your wrap-up, come back to the comment or present a different point of view in a positive way. But don't reprimand the student who voiced the comment.

DON'T BE THE AUTHORITATIVE ANSWER

Some kids think you have the right answer to every question. They'll look to you for approval, even when they are answering another group member's question. If they start to focus on you for answers, redirect them toward the group by making a comment like, "Remember that you're talking to everyone, not just me."

Your goal as the facilitator is to keep the discussion alive and kicking. It's important that your kids think of you as a member of the group—on their level. The less authoritative you are, the

more value your own opinions will have. If your kids view you as a peer, they will listen to your comments. You have a tremendous responsibility to be, with sincerity, their trusted friend.

LISTEN TO EACH PERSON

God gave you one mouth and two ears. Good discussion leaders know how to listen. Although it's tempting at times, don't monopolize the discussion. Encourage others to talk first— then express your opinions during your wrap up.

DON'T FORCE IT

Encourage all your kids to talk, but don't make them comment. Each member has the right to pass. If you feel that the discussion isn't going well, go on to the next question or restate the question to keep them moving.

DON'T TAKE SIDES

You'll probably have different opinions expressed in the group from time to time. Be extra careful not to take one side or another. Encourage both sides to think through their positions—ask questions to get them deeper. If everyone agrees on an issue, you can play devil's advocate with tough questions and stretch their thinking. Remain neutral—your point of view is your own, not that of the group.

DON'T LET ANYONE (INCLUDING YOU) TAKE OVER

Nearly every youth group has one person who likes to talk and is perfectly willing to express an opinion on any subject. Try to encourage equal participation from all the kids.

SET UP FOR THE TALK

Make sure that the seating arrangement is inclusive and encourages a comfortable, safe atmosphere for discussion. Theater-style seating (in rows) isn't discussion-friendly. Instead, arrange the chairs in a circle or semicircle (or on the floor with pillows!).

LET THEM LAUGH!

Discussions can be fun! Most of the TalkSheets include questions that'll make them laugh and get them thinking, too.

LET THEM BE SILENT

Silence can be a scary for discussion leaders! Some react by trying to fill the silence with a question or a comment. The following suggestions may help you to handle silence more effectively—

- Be comfortable with silence. Wait it out for 30 seconds or so to respond. You may want to restate the question to give your kids a gentle nudge.
- Talk about the silence with the group. What does the silence mean? Do they really not have any comments? Maybe they're confused, embarrassed, or don't want to share.
- Answer the silence with questions or comments like, "I know this is challenging to think about..." or "It's scary to be the first to talk." If you acknowledge the silence, it may break the ice.
- Ask a different question that may be easier to handle or that will clarify the one already posed. But don't do this too quickly without giving them time to think the first one through.

KEEP IT UNDER CONTROL

Monitor the discussion. Be aware if the discussion is going in a certain direction or off track. This can happen fast, especially if the kids disagree or things get heated. Mediate wisely and set the tone that you want. If your group gets bored with an issue, get them back on track. Let the discussion unfold, but be sensitive to your group and who is or is not getting involved.

If a student brings up a side issue that's interesting, decide whether or not to purse it. If discussion is going well and the issue is worth discussion, let them talk it through. But, if things get way off track, say something like, "Let's come back to that subject later if we have time. Right now, let's finish our discussion on..."

BE CREATIVE AND FLEXIBLE

You don't have to follow the order of the questions on the TalkSheet. Follow your own creative instinct. If you find other ways to use the TalkSheets, use them! Go ahead and add other questions or Bible references.

Don't feel pressured to spend time on every single activity. If you're short on time, you can skip some items. Stick with the questions that are the most interesting to the group.

SET YOUR GOALS

TalkSheets are designed to move along toward a goal, but you need to identify your goal in advance. What would you like your young people to learn? What truth should they discover? What is the goal of the session? If you don't know where you're going, it's doubtful you will get there.

BE THERE FOR YOUR KIDS

Some kids may want to talk more with you (you got 'em thinking!). Let them know that you can talk one-on-one with them afterwards.

Communicate to the kids that they can feel free to talk with you about anything with confidentiality. Let them know you're there for them with support and concern, even after the TalkSheet discussion has been completed.

USE THE BIBLE

Most adults believe the Bible has authority over their lives. It's common for adults to start their discussions or to support their arguments with Bible verses. But today's teenagers form their opinions and beliefs from their own life situations first—then they decide how the Bible fits their needs. TalkSheets start with the realities of the adolescent world and then move toward the Bible. You'll be able to show them that the Bible can be their guide and that God does have something to say to them about their own unique situations.

The last activity on each TalkSheet uses Bible verses that were chosen for their application to each issue. But they aren't exhaustive. Feel free to add whatever other verses you think would fit well and add to the discussion.

After your kids read the verses, ask them to think how the verses apply to their lives and summarize the meanings for them.

For example, after reading the passage for "Livin' It Up," you may summarize by saying something like, "See? God wants us to have fun! In fact, Jesus spoke in his parables of feasts, dancing, and celebration. It's obvious that God wants Christians to have good times—but to be careful, too."

CLOSE THE DISCUSSION

Present a challenge to the group by asking yourself, "What do I want the kids to remember most from this discussion?" There's your wrap-up! It's important to conclude by affirming the group and offering a summary that ties the discussion together.

Sometimes you won't need a wrap-up. You may want to leave the issue hanging and discuss it in another meeting. That way, your group can think about it more and you can nail down the final ideas later.

TAKE IT FURTHER

On the leader's guide page, you'll find additional discussion activities—labeled More—for following up on the discussion. These aren't a must, but highly recommended. They let the kids reflect upon, evaluate, review, and assimilate what they've learned. These activities may lead to more discussion and better learning.

After you've done the activity, be sure to debrief your kids on the activity, either now or at the next group meeting. A few good questions to ask about the activity are—

- What happened when you did this activity or discussion?

- Was it helpful or a waste of time?

- How did you feel when doing the activity or discussion?

- Did the activity/discussion make you think differently or affect you in any way?

- In one sentence state what you learned from this activity or discussion.

A FINAL WORD TO THE WISE — THAT'S YOU!

Some of these TalkSheets deal with topics that may be sensitive or controversial for your kids. Issues like sexuality or materialism aren't discussed openly in some churches. You're encouraging discussion and inviting your kids to express their opinions. As a result, you may be criticized by parents or others in your church who may not see the importance of such discussions. Use your best judgment. If you suspect that a particular TalkSheet will cause problems, you may not want to use it. Or you may want to tweak a particular TalkSheet and only cover some of the questions. Either way, the potential bad could outweigh the good—better safe than sorry. To avoid any misunderstanding, you may want to give the parents or senior pastor (or whoever else you are accountable to) copies of the TalkSheet before you use it. Let them know the discussion you would like to have and the goal you are hoping to accomplish. Challenge your kids to take their TalkSheet home to talk about it with their parents. How would their parents, as young people, have answered the questions? Your kids may find that their parents understand them better than they thought! Also, encourage them to think of other Bible verses or ways that the TalkSheet applies to their lives.

NOT WORTH LIVING

1. What do you think of when you hear the word **suicide**?

2. What do you think makes life worth living?

3. Below are five things that might cause someone your age to take his or her life. **Circle** the one that you think is the most common. What is one way to handle each of these problems other than suicide?
   a. Going through parents' divorce
   b. Thinking no one cares
   c. Breaking up with someone
   d. Being abused by a parent
   e. Feeling worthless and unimportant
   f. Failing their classes
   g. Not knowing what to do after high school

4. Jason's parents got divorced when he was nine—now he's 16. He feels unloved and unwanted by both parents. He sent you an e-mail saying he "just can't take it" and wants to die. You've known Jason for two years, but had no idea he felt this depressed. What can you do?
   ❑ Take the e-mail to a school counselor.
   ❑ Talk to my parents or guardians about it.
   ❑ Talk to my youth pastor about it.
   ❑ Laugh it off.
   ❑ Tell myself he didn't mean it—he only wanted attention.
   ❑ Delete it and forget about it.
   ❑ Tell Jason's parents.
   ❑ Call the police.
   ❑ Talk to Jason about his feelings.
   ❑ Pray for someone else to help him.
   ❑ Other—

5. Read each of the Bible verses below, and complete the statements in your own words.
Psalm 23:4-6	When I feel down, **God can**—
Galatians 6:2	I have a **responsibility** to—
Hebrews 4:15-16	**Christ understands** how I feel because—

From *High School TalkSheets—Updated!* by David Lynn. Permission to reproduce this page granted only for use in the buyer's own youth group. www.YouthSpecialties.com

11

NOT WORTH LIVING [s u i c i d e]

THIS WEEK

Suicide is a real and serious issue in the lives of teenagers today. Suicide is one of the top five causes of death among teenagers and young adults. Now more than ever, we must address the issues that lead to suicide, such as depression and loneliness.

Be sure to monitor this discussion carefully—this is a heavy issue in the lives of some teenagers. Be sensitive to your group members and their responses to the discussion.

OPEN

Start by having your kids make a list, either as a group or individually, of issues that teenagers deal with that get them down. Prompt them by asking questions like—what stresses them out, what pressures they face, or what makes them want to give up. List these issues and talk about which ones are the most difficult to deal with. Why might some people want to end their lives for these issues? How would your kids deal with these issues? What makes kids their age feel that theirs no way out?

THE DISCUSSION, BY NUMBERS

1. Have your kids list their thoughts on the word suicide. You may want to list these on a white-board or poster board. Be extra sensitive to the fact that some of them may have known and loved a person who has committed suicide. Your kids may have many emotional responses—from guilt and self-blame, to anger and resentment. Take the time to talk about each of these reactions to suicide.

2. You'll be able to learn a great deal about each of your kids and their beliefs from their response. You may want to make another list of what makes life worth living. What makes their lives exciting? What do they think the purpose of life is?

3. Discuss these reasons for suicide and ask your kids share some alternatives for dealing with them. Have them evaluate if the alternatives are effective or practical. Why or why not? Point out that there are alternatives—wanting out or escaping a problem doesn't fix it. Challenge your kids to stop and think about the problem. Is it worth ending their life over?

4. Use this tension-getter to talk about ways Christians should respond to a hurting person. Some of your kids might have different reactions. You may want to have them share them. Emphasize that even Christians deal with thoughts of suicide—they are not above feeling helpless, out of control, and depressed.

5. Ask your kids to share their sentences. Stress that our responsibility as Christians is to support and encourage others—even those who aren't in our group of friends.

THE CLOSE

In your wrap-up, be careful not to gloss over any problems or issues that your kids are facing. Their problems, like your problems, bring worry and concern. Using Hebrews 4:15-16, point out that Christ understands our every problem. He was human and he felt the same emotions we feel—he knows how we feel. Challenge your kids to lay out their problems and ask Christ for peace and strength.

Point out again that everyone has feelings of worthlessness and frustration. Encourage them to find someone to vent to—either a parent, teacher, counselor, pastor, or you.

Close with some suggestions about recognizing someone who is seriously in danger of taking his or her own life. What are some signs that your kids can look for? Visit a few online organizations for more information—Suicide Voices Awareness of Education (www.save.org) and the American Foundation for Suicide Prevention (www.afsp.org).

Finally, point out that depression and feelings of helplessness are not sinful. Depression is a clinically diagnosed disease that affects millions of adults and teenagers each year. Encourage them to talk with a trusted adult to find help. Visit the National Foundation For Depressive Illness, Inc. (www.depression.org) or find more information at www.depression.com.

MORE

● Ask your kids do some on-line research on suicide and depression. What can they find about teenage suicide, including causes and casualty rates among men and women? What are the types of depression, the causes of depression, and ways to cure depression?

● What do your kids hear or see in the media on depression and suicide? Maybe show a short clip of a TV show of a teenage problem and discuss ways to handle the problem. How does the media portray suicide and depression? What TV shows or movies have they seen that addresses these issues? What have they read or seen on the issues of suicide and how teenagers handle their struggles?

BELIEVING IT

1. Name a few people who you think have a **strong** faith in God.

2. What do you think of the following statements— do you **A (agree)** or **D (disagree)**?

   ___ Faith will take away all your doubts forever.
   ___ Faith is a crutch for most people.
   ___ Faith isn't easy to have today, like it was in Bible times.
   ___ Faith will help me pass my math exam.
   ___ Faith isn't required by God all the time.
   ___ Faith would come easier for me if I saw a miracle.
   ___ Faith will heal you when you are sick.
   ___ Faith will make everything in your life easier.

3. How much does your faith in Christ affect each of things listed? Rate these from **not very affected (1)** to **very affected (10)**.

   ___ Friends   ___ Work
   ___ Family   ___ School
   ___ Extra curricular activities   ___ Free time
   ___ Thoughts   ___ Self-esteem
   ___ Dating   ___ Future plans

4. Below are a few statements of Christian faith. Which ones do you believe completely **(circle these)**? Which ones do you have doubts about **(put a question mark by these)**?

   a. I believe in God.
   b. I believe Christ rose from the dead.
   c. I believe the Bible is true.
   d. I believe I will go to heaven when I die.
   e. I believe God answers prayer.

   f. I believe that God loves all people equally.
   g. I believe that the Holy Spirit lives in me.
   h. I believe that I'm a sinner.
   i. I believe in Jesus Christ.
   j. I believe that hell is a reality.

5. Check out the Bible verses below, and complete the sentences in your own words.

   Romans 10:17   Faith comes from—
   Hebrews 11:1   Faith is—
   Hebrews 12:2   Jesus is—
   James 2:18-19   Faith is shown by—

BELIEVING IT [f a i t h]

THIS WEEK

High school brings a lot of change to the lives of teenagers. Some will question their beliefs as they think about the world they live in. And they may question the beliefs of their parents or other adults in their lives. Some may be confused about their faith in God. Others may reject the faith that they've been raised in. This session allows your group to discuss the concept of faith and what it means to Christians.

OPEN

Start this session off by having your group make two separate lists on a whiteboard or poster board—one list of things that they can be sure of, another of things that they can't be sure of. For example, they can be sure that the sky is blue, that milk comes from cows, and that fire is hot. But they can't be sure of things like when the world will end, when they'll die, or who they'll marry.

Now go through both lists and put check marks next to those that we have control of as humans (for instance, "I know that I will fail if I don't study). Then star those that others have control of ("I don't know if my teacher likes me"). Finally, circle those that God is in charge of (basically everything).

Ask your group which ones are scary to them—usually the ones they aren't sure of. What are they scared of? How do they feel knowing that they have no control over situations? What is hard about believing in something you can't see? You'll probably get answers like "because I doubt it" or "because you can't prove it." How do they feel knowing that someone has control of circumstances? Finally, what do they think faith is? Is it only believing in God or can you have faith in other things, like people or events?

THE DISCUSSION, BY NUMBERS

1. Ask each of your kids why they chose the people they listed. How can they tell that they have a strong faith? What characteristics do they have? What kind of relationship do they think these people have with God?

2. Each of these statements examines faith from a different angle. Let your kids share their choices and why they chose them. You may want to keep your opinions until the close of the session.

3. This will get your kids thinking about how their faith affects their lives. Don't make them share their ratings—maybe ask the group to rate them together, based on their answers and those of teenagers in general.

4. These will help your kids examine and reflect on their beliefs. You may also use these statements to start a discussion on the basic beliefs of the Christian faith. If so, you might want to pass out copies of the Apostles' Creed or your church's statement of faith for review. Use this time to affirm the things that your kids believe in strongly. Communicate that having doubts is normal and human—even John the Baptist had doubts, as is described in Luke 7:18-19.

5. Have some of your kids volunteer to read the sentences aloud. Or have them write them out on a large piece of white paper or poster board. Discuss each of the verses and then talk about each passage, its context, and what it says about having faith.

THE CLOSE

Having doubts is normal—in fact, people often grow in our faith through their doubts. Challenge your group to think about what they believe—outside the beliefs of their parents. Ask them to examine how faith and beliefs relate to their everyday lives. What changes does their faith make, if any? How do they incorporate faith into their everyday lives? Point out that the Bible teaches that faith without works is dead (James 2:14-17)—what does this mean to them? What kind of actions does faith lead to?

Close with a time of prayer and give your group time for silent prayer. Challenge them to think about their beliefs and what God means to them. If you sense that some group members may not know the gospel of Christ, use this time to go through the plan of salvation. Remind them that God is waiting with open arms—he loves them more than they know.

MORE

● Hold a faith Q & A time with your group. Have the group write down any questions they have about the Christian faith on 3x5 cards (anonymously). Then collect the cards and have your kids take turns picking out questions. If they feel comfortable, have them try to answer it or pass it on. Discuss the questions as a group and encourage them to use the Bible for back up to their questions and answers. To liven things up, invite your senior pastor to a meeting and put him in the hot seat for a question and answer session!

● Have your kids e-mail or talk with one adult this week about their belief in God, life after death, the Bible, miracles, prayer, and so on. This could be a parent, relative, teacher, or adult friend.

FEELING THE HEAT

1. What are the three most common sources for information on **sex**?
   - ❑ The Bible
   - ❑ Friends
   - ❑ Sex ed classes
   - ❑ Doctors
   - ❑ Pastors and youth leaders
   - ❑ Magazines or books
   - ❑ Teachers
   - ❑ Parents or guardians
   - ❑ Family planning clinics
   - ❑ Radio talk shows
   - ❑ Movies and television
   - ❑ The Internet
   - ❑ Other—

2. What do these sources emphasize **most** about sex?

   Parents—

   Internet—

   Church—

   Friends—

   Television and Movies—

   Magazines—

3. Lara's school counselor told her she should take birth control if she's been dating a guy regularly, just in case. The counselor gave her the name of a clinic where she could get the Pill.

   a. What do you think of the counselor's advice?

   b. What should Lara do?

   c. Is it wrong for Lara to be taking birth control?

   d. Does taking the Pill give her an excuse to have sex?

   e. What advice would you give Lara?

4. What "lines" do people use in order to pressure someone into having premarital sex? (For example, "Don't worry, I've got condoms.") Are these lines effective? Why or why not?

5. Check out one of the following Bible passages and write your response in one sentence.

   1 Corinthians 6:18-20

   Ephesians 5:1-3

   1 Thessalonians 4:3-8

FEELING THE HEAT [premarital sex]

THIS WEEK

Sex is everywhere. Advertisements, TV shows, magazines, and movies all tell teenagers that premarital sex is accepted—and normal. Your kids need to hear the other side of the story in a positive, nonjudgmental way. This TalkSheet allows you to address premarital sex and sexuality in a Christian context—without lecturing or preaching at your kids.

Try to be extra careful that you, and your adult volunteers, keep a neutral stance and don't come off as judgmental during this discussion. Your goal is to discuss the meaning of sex in a healthy way, not to condemn any kids who may be sexually active.

OPEN

Whatever you do for your intro, communicate that sex is a normal, healthy part of a loving, committed relationship. Our society has warped its meaning—that's why you're going to talk about it!

Start by asking them why God created sex. What have your kids been told about sex in the church? Read in the Bible? Then ask the group to list where sex is shown, talked about, referred to, sung about, and so on in the media. Make a master list of these on a poster or whiteboard if you wish. How was sex was portrayed? Was is good? Bad? Dirty? Uncomfortable? How has that media warped the meaning of sex?

THE DISCUSSION, BY NUMBERS

1. What are the three most common sources of information about sex? Most likely, they won't include parents or church. Point out that knowledge on sex is usually based on misleading information from the media. What sources would they like to get more information from? What is the most dependable?

2. Draw up a master list of all the messages. Ask them which are true or false, which are good or bad, and which are consistent with the teachings of the Bible.

3. This tension-getter will most likely get a lot of different opinions. The questions assume the couple will have sex, so be prepared. Ask your kids if this assumption is true of their peers. In general terms, do most teenagers deal with these issues? As a Christian how would they handle the situation?

4. Let the group share their responses to these lines. These statements or lines are about using people—pressuring someone into sex for selfish reasons and not for the other person's benefit. What does this say about respecting another

person's body and beliefs? How would a Christian resisting this pressure? Is it easier? Harder?

5. Focusing on what God wants Christians to do sexually, ask them to share their thoughts. Point out the fact God isn't depriving us of sex. It's the opposite—he wants only the best for us physically, emotionally, socially, and spiritually. God understands their struggles, he knows, and he can keep them strong.

THE CLOSE

Summarize the points that have been covered, but focus on God's forgiveness. Many of your kids have probably already done things they regret and feel guilty about. You may wish to read a few verses about God's forgiveness and compassion—Isaiah 1:18 or 1 John 1:9. It's never too late to get right with God and start over.

Emphasize your willingness to talk to group members about sexual topics they may need to discuss privately and confidentially. If your kids are victims of inappropriate comments, touches, or sexual aggression—or suspect others are—they must get help immediately from a school counselor, parent, pastor, or you. For more information, visit the Rape, Abuse, and Incest National Network (www.rainn.org) or National Coalition Against Sexual Assault (http://ncasa.org).

MORE

● You may want to take some time to talk about sexual pornography in magazines and on the Internet. Pornography is a drug—a very addictive habit—and it damages relationships. It is crucial that those within your group who struggle with pornography or have friends who do get help immediately.

● Challenge your kids to start praying for their future spouses now! Have them bring their future husbands and wives before God to have him prepare their hearts, minds, and bodies for marriage.

THE DATING GAME

1. If you could go on the **ideal date**, what would it be? Where would you go?

2. Which **three** of the following characteristics would you choose to describe your ideal guy or girl?
   - ❑ They can be open and honest with me.
   - ❑ They treat me with respect, as if I'm special.
   - ❑ They will listen when I need to talk.
   - ❑ They're popular.
   - ❑ They won't date anyone else but me.
   - ❑ They're very good-looking.
   - ❑ They like to try new and different things.
   - ❑ They're very intelligent and get good grades.
   - ❑ The're involved in church activities.
   - ❑ They want to get physical right away.
   - ❑ They have a lot of money.
   - ❑ They're a strong Christian.
   - ❑ They have a sense of humor.

3. What do you think? **D (definitely)**, **M (maybe)**, or **N (never)**
   - ___ A person should date as many people as he or she can.
   - ___ Christians should pray together on a date.
   - ___ The best age to begin dating is 16.
   - ___ Heavy petting is okay as long as the couple doesn't go all the way.
   - ___ Christians should date only other Christians.
   - ___ It's okay for a girl to ask a guy for a date.
   - ___ The purpose of dating is to prepare for marriage.
   - ___ You should only date people your parents or guardians approve of.
   - ___ Couples should share expenses on a date.
   - ___ It is wrong for homosexuals to date.

4. What do each of these passages say about dating?
   1 Kings 11:1-4
   1 Corinthians 5:9-11
   Galatians 5:16

THE DATING GAME [dating]

THIS WEEK

Society and the media pressures teenagers to date at a young age—and to experiment with physical intimacy. These pressures are making an impact on Christian youth today—when they date, who they date, and how to handle social and sexual issues. This TalkSheet provides a forum to discuss dating and how to handle it from God's perspective.

OPEN

To quickly break the ice with your kids, you may want to share a humorous anecdote from your own dating history or ask several of your leaders to share stories of their own (changing names to protect the innocent!) Then have the group vote and give an award for the worst date story.

Or you can also find funny dating stories from magazines (almost every teenage magazine has them) and compare these. You kids may be able to find some of their own examples in magazines or from personal experience. Have them write out their experiences on paper and read them out loud (anonymously, of course!).

THE DISCUSSION, BY NUMBERS

1. Your kids will have different ideas on this! List them on a whiteboard, in case you want to refer to them later.

2. This forces your kids to assess their priorities and their values, because they're limited to three choices. You may want to tally up the votes for each trait to find out what the group thinks is most important. Ask your adult leaders to give some input as well.

3. Use this activity to let the group argue and debate the issue. You may want to divide them into groups, give them time to formulate a case for their position, and then let the teams state their case. Encourage them to use the Bible for support and to share any verses they found relating to the issue.

4. Dating isn't mentioned specifically in the Bible, so your kids will practice applying the Bible to modern life. Have them share their interpretations of each verse, then give your own comments to a passage or two along with a practical application.

THE CLOSE

Dating is a huge part of the teenage life. There's so much pressure to date—but it's okay (and healthy!) to not date. Communicate that dating is about building healthy relationships with others—it's not about who dates the most or gets the most "action" on dates. Dating doesn't have to be romantic—it can simply be having fun with others and building relationships. Ask your group why some people feel that they're a loser if they don't date. Why or why not? Why is their so much emphasis on dating?

You may also want to talk about the pressures of physical intimacy that come with dating. What is good or bad about dating someone for a long time? How do teenagers in general handle sexual relationships in general? How is this different among Christian kids?

Finally, you may want to close in prayer with your group. Challenge them to ask God for wisdom and self-control in their dating. Point out that God is in control of their relationships and expects them to be respectful towards the other person who they are with. Challenge them to start praying now for their future husbands and wives, asking God to prepare the other person for them and their relationship.

MORE

● Cases of date rape and physical abuse are on the rise. You may want to discuss safe ways to date without getting in a bad situation. Point out that date rape is a crime—no one, under no circumstances, can force another person into sex. What are ways to protect themselves from becoming a victim? Encourage them to meet the person if they don't feel comfortable riding in the same car and to date in social places where there are other people. Finally, communicate that if they are ever hit, pressured into sex, or raped, they must find a trusted adult to talk to—you, a pastor, teacher, counselor or parent. For more information, visit the Rape, Abuse, and Incest National Network (www.rainn.org) or National Coalition Against Sexual Assault (http://ncasa.org).

● What does our society say about dating? There are articles on the Internet and in several teenage magazines (such as *Seventeen*, *YM*, and *Mademoiselle*) on dating. Ask your kids to find some statistics, questions and answers, or articles on dating and the risks involved. Then discuss the articles and what happened. How can Christians handle situations like this? How can your kids encourage their friends and peers to date in healthy ways?

HUGS AND KISSES

1. What does the word **love** mean to you?

2. **Circle** the words below that you think best describe love.

Romance	Sharing	Adoration	Lust
Sex	Responsibility	Vulnerability	Marriage
Forever	Giving	Admiration	Kissing
Fun	Passion	Devotion	Friendship
Commitment	Infatuation	Idealism	Other—

3. Most girls Chandra's age are trying to find a guy to fall in love with. Chandra, a junior in high school, has a different sort of problem. She's trying to get her old boyfriend, Gabriel, to fall out of love with her. He won't give up, saying he can't get her out of his mind and still loves her.

   What advice would you give **Chandra**?

   What advice would you have for **Gabriel**?

4. It was just like a movie—Antonio and Erika met while skiing in Colorado. Now, only three months later, Antonio has asked Erika to marry him. She says she wants to marry Antonio—even though he's six years older and has been married before. After all, she's in love with him, and that's all that matters.

   What advice would you give **Erika**?

   What advice would you give **Antonio**?

   What advice would their **parents** give?

5. What do you think—yes or no?
   ___ True love can conquer all.
   ___ True love is something you feel in your heart.
   ___ True love is blind.
   ___ True love happens only once in a lifetime.
   ___ True love lasts forever.
   ___ True love makes premarital sex okay.
   ___ True love doesn't happen at first sight.
   ___ True love only happens in the movies.

6. Which one of the following Bible stories do you think describes **true love?**
   Genesis 29:18-20   2 Samuel 11:2-5
   Judges 14:1-3   Esther 2:17

From *High School TalkSheets—Updated!* by David Lynn. Permission to reproduce this page granted only for use in the buyer's own youth group. www.YouthSpecialties.com

19

HUGS AND KISSES [r o m a n t i c   l o v e]

THIS WEEK

Your kids may have mixed ideas about what love is. The media portrays romantic love as warm fuzzy moments while kissing and cuddling. A lot of teenagers think love is a feeling. Others think it's physical attraction or sexual intimacy. The purpose of this TalkSheet is to discuss what love really means. Jesus taught that love was more than a feeling—and he lived it! It's an action, a commitment, and a way of life.

OPEN

Send your group on a Love Scavenger Hunt. For example—how many titles of new release movies does Blockbuster (or some other video store) have with *love* in the title? How many magazines have the word *love* on the front cover? How many current radio songs are there with *love* in the title or that talk about love? What CDs do they have that have *love* in the lyrics or title? Have them bring specific examples of titles or lyrics. Use your creativity and use what time you have. Then talk about what they learned from finding these.

THE DISCUSSION, BY NUMBERS

1. Have your kids share what they think love is. Encourage them use the words from item 2 as a springboard. Write these on a master list on a whiteboard or poster board. You'll use this list later on.

2. Have them share their choices and add these to your list from question 1. Be careful not to judge the words they've chosen. Ask why they have chosen the ones they did. Does the rest of the group agree or disagree? Why or why not?

3. & 4. These tension-getters offer an opportunity to discuss true love versus feelings of love. You may want to discuss them from different angles. For example in the first scenario suppose Chandra was not a Christian, or was pregnant, or had fallen in love with another guy. In the second scenario you could suppose Erika is only 16 or that both Antonia and Erika are Christians. As you give each variable to the kids, ask them if it would make any difference in their advice. Why or why not? Another idea is to divide the kids into smaller groups, giving each one of these situations. Let them decide what should be done, then present and discuss their conclusions with the rest of the group.

5. Talk over each statement and let the kids debate them. What are the different opinions? Do they agree with each other? Why or why not? Point out that girls and guys may have different opinions. Some of the items may bring up the subject of divorce. Remember to be sensitive when discussing this issue—several in the group may have divorced parents.

6. Allow the kids to read and reflect on each of these stories and share their opinions of them. Point out that not all Bible characters were perfect. What does the story say about love?

THE CLOSE

Using your list from items 1 and 2, make another list of what love is according to God. Using 1 Corinthians 13:1-13, make a list of what love is and isn't—what does love mean in everyday life through our actions? Challenge them to give specific examples of how to show love. Then, encourage them to think of one area of love that they need to work on. Who do they need to try harder to love? What actions to they need to change?

Focus on and discuss the three kinds of love the Greeks described: agape, phileo and eros. Agape is God's love for us—a genuine, sacrificial love that is unselfish and giving. Phileo is friendship love. Eros is love on a more physical, sexual level. Concentrate on agape, the love Christ exemplified. Healthy marriages and relationships involve all three types of love. Communicate that love is much more than a feeling of infatuation or romance. It involves responsibility and commitment. It's a decision, an act of will.

MORE

● Divide the kids into groups and have them each find (or you can do this beforehand) and research the lyrics of a popular love song—most can be easily obtained on the Internet. Then examine what it implies about love. What is it saying? How would they evaluate the song based on the discussion of love? What does the song mean to a Christian? How is it different?

● What is sacrificial love? You may ask the group to find examples of sacrificial love in the Bible. What characters showed agape love? What did they do? What did God say or would've said? Point out that agape love means swallowing our pride and sacrificing ourselves! It must have been for Christ to give it up and die for us. If he could do that for us, think of all the smaller things we can do!

LOVING FOR A LIFETIME

1. Check what you think is the **best** age for marriage.

   Women
   - ❏ 15-18
   - ❏ 19-22
   - ❏ 23-26
   - ❏ 27-30
   - ❏ over 30

   Men
   - ❏ 15-18
   - ❏ 19-22
   - ❏ 23-26
   - ❏ 27-30
   - ❏ over 30

2. Rank the following issues in marriage from the **most important (1)** to the least **important (12)**.

   ___ Sex
   ___ Children
   ___ Communication
   ___ Commitment

   ___ Religion
   ___ Mutual interests
   ___ Financial security
   ___ Respect

   ___ Faithfulness
   ___ Romantic love
   ___ Friendship
   ___ Loyalty

3. Which of the following best describes how you feel about couples **living together** before marriage?
   - ❏ It's totally acceptable.
   - ❏ It's a good way to see if a marriage will work.
   - ❏ It's better than getting a divorce later.
   - ❏ It's permissible if you are an adult.
   - ❏ It's totally unacceptable.
   - ❏ It saves paying oodles in rent.

4. Choose 10 of the following qualities that you would like your future spouse to have, ranking them from **most important (1)** to **least important (10)**.

   ___ Good looks
   ___ Money
   ___ Fantastic body
   ___ Intelligence
   ___ Good parenting potential
   ___ Assertive
   ___ Emotionally healthy
   ___ Similar values

   ___ Sense of humor
   ___ Shared interests
   ___ Commitment to Christ
   ___ Honesty and trustworthiness
   ___ Respectful of you
   ___ Leadership abilities
   ___ Good income

   ___ Considerate and caring
   ___ Good sex partner
   ___ Communication skills
   ___ Romantic and loving
   ___ A good friend
   ___ A nice family

5. What do these verses say about **marriage** and **love**?
   Proverbs 18:22   1 Corinthians 7:1-11   2 Corinthians 6:14-16

LOVING FOR A LIFETIME [marriage]

THIS WEEK

Face it—society's view of marriage is deteriorating. Marriage problems abound. More and more couples are living together without getting married. It's no wonder that teenagers may question the purpose and meaning of marriage. This TalkSheet gives your group the opportunity to discuss the truth about marriage, within a Christian context and from a Christian perspective—and clear up the misconceptions, low expectations, and false ideals that society has given them.

OPEN

Whether you are married or not, start out by presenting this case scenario to role play with your group. You are a 20 year old girl or guy. You've just broken up (for good) with the love of your life who you thought was "the one." Now you're questioning what marriage is all about and why anyone would ever want to get married. Why do you want to keep dating to find someone else? What should your reasons for marriage be?

Have your kids brainstorm their ideas and write down a master list on a whiteboard or poster board of the reasons for marriage. Some will be straight up obvious (companionship, sex) and some won't be ("someone to cook for you"). Have them list everything they think of when they hear the word marriage and why marriage beats living together beforehand.

THE DISCUSSION, BY NUMBERS

1. Ask your kids share their choices and why they chose the age they did. What are the pros and cons of each age group?

2. Discuss the three most popular answers and the three least popular answers. Encourage your group to debate these answers. Why or why not they are important? What reasoning do they have for each? Then rank them again as a group on a poster board or whiteboard.

3. Living together is a popular alternative to marriage today. Many young people have been affected by divorce or their parents live in boyfriends or girlfriends. Many are scared of marriage as a result. Debate the pros and cons of living together, and challenge them to give their honest opinions. Save yours—and biblical beliefs—for the closing statement.

4. Allow the group to debate their preferred traits with each other. You may want to make a master list of the favorites and discuss them further.

Have them rank which ones are the least important to most important.

5. Go through these passages to hear which ones they picked and how they summarized them. What did the passages teach them about love and marriage?

THE CLOSE

Share a brief biblical view of marriage. Communicate that that despite the failures of today's marriages, it is holy and instituted by God—it shouldn't be taken lightly. Marriage is one of life's most important of decisions, and—with God's help—marriage can be successful.

Go back to your list from the intro and compare their list with God's intentions for marriage. Point out that God created marriage for all those good things—all those bonuses that come along with having a forever friend. Have any of them changed their idea of what marriage is?

Challenge your kids to think seriously about what they are looking for in a marriage partner. How can they start today to think about healthy marriages? What can they learn from society's mistakes and portrayal of marriage and divorce?

Finally, encourage those who have experienced the pain of divorce to forgive their parents and give their hurt to Christ. Point out that Christ can heal broken and hurting relationships—he's there for them with open arms. And, be sure your kids know that you are available to talk more one-on-one.

MORE

● Have a group that's more visual? Show clips of or have each of your kids watch a TV show with a married couple in it. How is marriage portrayed? Is it good and bad? What problems or arguments did they have? Have them discuss their conclusions and how media portrays marriage as opposed to reality.

● Or have a Q & A session with a married couple or a divorced person to openly discuss their marriage experiences and have your kids ask questions about how to handle dating, communication, and life as a couple. Try to keep your kids on track with the larger issues (not just sex questions). Finally, challenge your kids to ask their parents about being married, and encourage them to support their parents who may be going through marriage struggles.

TO DO OR NOT TO DO

1. Do behaviors fall in line with your values and beliefs? Rate yourself on a scale of 1-10 (1 being "my behaviors don't reflect my values at all" and 10 being "my behaviors match my values all the time").

2. When you think that something is **wrong**, but you go ahead and do it anyway—
How do you feel?

Why did you choose to do it?

Do you feel guilty later?

3. What would you like to change **most** about your behaviors and values?

4. Last night Blake was supposed to help his youth group leader plan for the upcoming year of activities. But then his friend Deon called and said that the guys were going out drinking for Ryan's 18th birthday—and telling their parents they were having a study group. Blake wanted to go—Deon and Ryan were his best buddies. And it's not like he had to help plan for youth group next year. He could do it some other time. Bill called his youth leader and lied, saying that he had to study for the math test that he had forgotten about. His youth leader understood—but the next day called to see how the math test went.

What do you think of Blake's decision?

What would you do if you were Blake?

What advice would you have for Blake?

What would you think if you were the youth leader and you found out the truth?

5. Read the following Bible verses, and rate yourself on the scale of **1–10** (**1 = you're on track** and **10 = you need to work on this**).
    ___ Luke 6:46-47   ___ Romans 7:15   ___ Romans 14:22
    ___ Galatians 5:16   ___ 1 John 1:9

What do these verses say about Godly **values** and **behaviors**?

TO DO OR NOT TO DO [values and behavior]

THIS WEEK

The adolescent years are when teenagers are questioning their values and beliefs the most. They watch TV, listen to the radio, surf the Internet, and hang out with friends—influences that shape their values and behaviors. No wonder it's challenging for some to shape Christian values and live them! This TalkSheet will help you discuss how to shape Christian values and live them day in and day out.

OPEN

Have your guys sit or stand together in a huge human knot. Have them lock their arms and legs. Then let the girls try to pull them apart. A few rules, though—no hitting, pinching, or kicking—only pulling. Give them a few minutes. Then, debrief with your group to talk about struggles. What was hard about trying to pull them apart? Was it hard for the guys to stick together when they were being pulled away? Did the girls want to give up? What made the guys stick together so tightly?

Point out that some people make choices and stick with them but can be pulled away from these values. Like the human knot, it's important to surround yourself with people who have the same values and can hold each other accountable.

THE DISCUSSION, BY NUMBERS

1. How did your kids rate themselves? Explain to the group that the longer a person's behavior is inconsistent with his beliefs, the more his beliefs will change to match his behavior.

2. The kids may describe feelings of guilt in answer to this exercise. Make certain they understand that guilt isn't always bad—it was designed by God to pull our behavior patterns in line with our value system. When we stop feeling guilty for the inconsistency in our lives, then we're in serious trouble.

3. If sharing the sentences is uncomfortable, pass out 3x5 cards and have them write their responses. Collect the cards and read them aloud for discussion. Brainstorm practical ways to change incompatible behavior patterns.

4. Discuss this tension-getter. Ask the group to rate Blake's actions on a scale of one (worst) to 10 (best). Most will choose a middle-of-the scale number. Point out that life is rarely divided into nice, safe categories where all our choices are obvious and easy to make—like a simple one or a 10. Sometimes they fall in the middle—the gray area—not clearly black or white. Ask them to describe similar situations they have experienced and what they did in each case.

5. Have the group look up each passage and allow the kids to evaluate where they stand on each one. If kids feel that they fall short of what God wants, help them to see that even a little improvement over time is better than no improvement at all.

THE CLOSE

Encourage your kids to think through their values and then try to live consistently with them. They need to walk their talk. You might choose a value everyone respects—such as loving our neighbors—and brainstorm a list of pertinent actions to be completed during the next week. Find methods of putting good values into consistent practice. The more frequently right choices are made, the easier they will be.

Encourage the kids to use the Bible for help and guidance. Suggest that they also ask parents and other Christians for advice when they are having difficulty making decisions. Let them know you yourself are anxious to help them, at any time.

MORE

● You may want to have your group search the Bible for stories of characters who struggled with decisions. A few of them include Adam and Eve (Genesis 3), Abraham (Genisis 12), Esau (Genesis 25:27), David (2 Samuel 11-12), and Matthew (Matthew 9:9). Ask your kids to study the way the situations were handled and how they were resolved. How did the characters' decisions affect their lives and the future of their families? How do these stories apply to the lives of your kids today?

● You may want to take some time to talk about values in the media. Make a list of values that your kids see on TV, in the movies, on the Internet, on the radio, etc. How do these values compare to the values Christians live by? In what ways do your kids face these values at school or at home? What can they do to resist these pressures? How much do your kids believe what they see and hear? Challenge them to keep their eyes open to contradicting values.

THE SUNDAY SITUATION

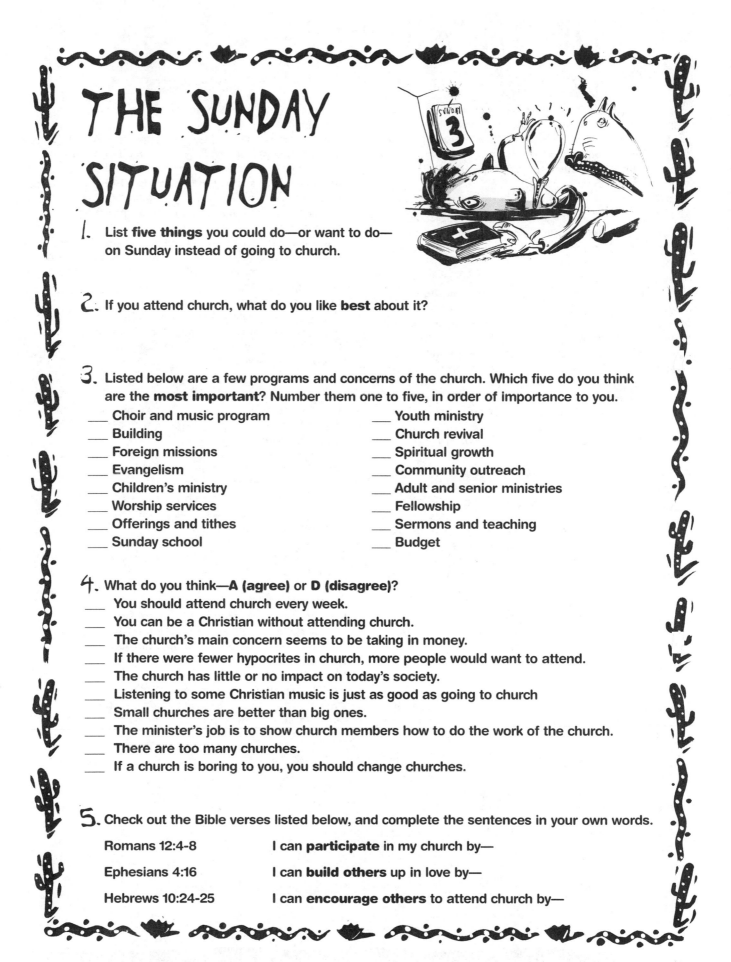

1. List **five things** you could do—or want to do—on Sunday instead of going to church.

2. If you attend church, what do you like **best** about it?

3. Listed below are a few programs and concerns of the church. Which five do you think are the **most important**? Number them one to five, in order of importance to you.

___ Choir and music program
___ Building
___ Foreign missions
___ Evangelism
___ Children's ministry
___ Worship services
___ Offerings and tithes
___ Sunday school

___ Youth ministry
___ Church revival
___ Spiritual growth
___ Community outreach
___ Adult and senior ministries
___ Fellowship
___ Sermons and teaching
___ Budget

4. What do you think—**A (agree)** or **D (disagree)**?
___ You should attend church every week.
___ You can be a Christian without attending church.
___ The church's main concern seems to be taking in money.
___ If there were fewer hypocrites in church, more people would want to attend.
___ The church has little or no impact on today's society.
___ Listening to some Christian music is just as good as going to church
___ Small churches are better than big ones.
___ The minister's job is to show church members how to do the work of the church.
___ There are too many churches.
___ If a church is boring to you, you should change churches.

5. Check out the Bible verses listed below, and complete the sentences in your own words.

Romans 12:4-8   I can **participate** in my church by—

Ephesians 4:16   I can **build others** up in love by—

Hebrews 10:24-25   I can **encourage others** to attend church by—

THE SUNDAY SITUATION [church]

THIS WEEK

What is the importance of going to church? Do you feel that some of your kids go just because their parents make them? This TalkSheet is designed to create discussion about the church and will encourage your high schoolers to get involved in it.

OPEN

You may want to start by asking the group to list all the churches that they know of or have been to. This can include different denominations, religions, and styles of worship. There are hundreds of different branches of churches—both Protestant and Catholic. Make a list of these suggestions and ask the group what makes a church. Is it a building? Is church a group of people? Can church be meeting with some friends together on a Sunday night?

Then ask your group what makes a church? Is it worship alone? What does going to church mean to them? Encourage them to be honest with their answers—some kids may not like church much. You may be surprised at the variety of answers.

THE DISCUSSION, BY NUMBERS

1. How did the group answer this question? Talk about the importance or unimportance of each activity in relationship to church attendance.

2. Ask the kids to list all the things they like about the church, keeping track of them on the whiteboard or poster board. Ask if there is anything they don't like and list them as well, but be careful this doesn't turn into a gripe session.

3. Put them in charge for once! What if they were on the church board to determine priorities for the church. What ministries they would discontinue, which they would keep, and which they would emphasize more?

   You might want to try this hypothetical situation—a rich widow dies and leaves $3 million to the church; how would your mock church board use the money?

4. Have a vote on each of the statements, according to their answers. If everyone agreed on a particular one, go on to the next. If there is a wide difference of opinion, discuss the pros and cons.

5. Read each passage and allow them to share their completed sentences with the group.

THE CLOSE

The following are some suggestions to emphasize as you close—

• The church is the body of Christ and everyone is a part of it. Christ is no longer physically present in the world, but his body, the church, is. When you become a Christian, you become part of that body. There is no such thing as a solitary Christian. Christians grow in community with each other.

• The purpose of church isn't entertainment. In a worship service, people aren't the audience—God is. Christians come to worship him and to grow closer to him. That requires expending some effort on their part.

• Young people aren't the church of tomorrow—they are the church of today! Your kids know that they are a vitally important part of the church. Encourage them to get involved.

MORE

● Want to see how much your kids know about their church? Make up a short quiz with questions about the church such as—

⇨ Name a missionary our church sponsors and the country where he or she serves.

⇨ What is our pastor's middle name?

⇨ What is the name of the church's newsletter?

⇨ Summarize last Sunday's (or this morning's) sermon in 25 words or less.

⇨ What year was our church founded?

⇨ Which family in our church has been a member the longest?

● Some of your kids may never have been to a church of a different denomination or religion. If you feel it's appropriate, attend a different worship service with some of your kids. Check out a non-denominational church or a Catholic mass. How do these church services differ from yours? Is it good or bad? What did the group like or not like? What did this experience teach them about the church and how God would view different denominations and styles of worship?

GOT SPIRIT?

1. What is the first thing you think of when you hear some one talk about the **Holy Spirit**?

2. How would you explain the **Holy Spirit** to a friend?

3. **Check** the things below you think the Holy Spirit can do for you.
   - ❏ Give you power to live a successful Christian life
   - ❏ Help you study
   - ❏ Teach you and help you mature as a Christian
   - ❏ Give you spiritual gifts
   - ❏ Make you better than others
   - ❏ Convict you of sin
   - ❏ Live inside of you
   - ❏ Give you peace and comfort
   - ❏ Help you make the right decisions
   - ❏ Take away your problems
   - ❏ Keep bad things from happening to you
   - ❏ Be your conscience
   - ❏ Give you love for people you don't like
   - ❏ Give you hope
   - ❏ Make you feel good inside
   - ❏ Other—

4. In the second chapter of the book of Acts, the Holy Spirit came to the disciples at Pentecost in a dramatic way. How do you think the Holy Spirit comes to people today?

5. Check out these verses, and then answer the questions.

   Galatians 5:22-26   Which fruit of the Spirit you **need most** in your life right now?

   John 14:17   How can you know **what** the Holy Spirit is?

   Romans 8:26   How does the Holy Spirit **help you** in prayer?

   Acts 2:2   **Where** does the Holy Spirit come from?

From *High School TalkSheets—Updated!* by David Lynn. Permission to reproduce this page granted only for use in the buyer's own youth group. www.YouthSpecialties.com

27

GOT SPIRIT? [Holy Spirit]

THIS WEEK

Some of your kids can relate to God the Father and God the Son—but what about God the Holy Spirit? It's hard to understand why or how God can be three different people at the same time. This TalkSheet gives you the chance to discuss the role the Holy Spirit plays in the life of a Christian.

OPEN

The Holy Spirit is a storehouse of power who can enable your kids to live the Christian life. To illustrate this point and introduce this session, empty a small pressurized can of shaving cream onto a table in front of the group. Look at how much a small container can hold! Point out something similar is true for the Holy Spirit living in us. As Christians, we have the power of God's Holy Spirit inside us—waiting to be released.

To get a bit deeper, ask the group how they can know the Spirit. How does God use the Spirit in their lives from day to day? Can they feel him? See him? What makes the Spirit different from Jesus? Or different from God?

THE DISCUSSION, BY NUMBERS

1. On a whiteboard or poster board, list all the words or phrases that the group listed. Why did they choose the ones they did?

2. How would your kids explain the concept of the Holy Spirit? Try to arrive at a definition of the Holy Spirit with your group. This definition should include the fact that God the Holy Spirit is as real and as important as God the Father or God the Son. You may want to consult your church's statement of faith or look up some of the following Scripture passages: John 14:15-31, Romans 8:1-17, 1 Corinthians 2:6-16.

3. Invite your group to share their choices. While all of the items on the list are things that the Holy Spirit can do, you may want to emphasize the things that are mentioned specifically in Scripture: comforts (John 14:16-17); convicts of sin, (John 16:8-11); teaches and guides (John 16:13); prays for us (Romans 8:26); gives spiritual gifts (1 Corinthians 12:7); leads (Galatians 5:18). If possible, take this opportunity to share specific examples of how you have experienced or witnessed the work of the Holy Spirit in your life. Ask some of the young people to do the same.

4. Read Acts 2:1-4, then have the group discuss their opinions. Other references in Scripture you may want to consider are Acts 4:8; 6:3-5; 9:17; 11:24; 13:9, 52; 1 Corinthians 12:13; or Ephesians 5:18.

5. What do these verses say about the Holy Spirit? Do they think differently of the Holy Spirit? Why or why not? You may want to ask for volunteers to share their sentences.

THE CLOSE

The Holy Spirit plays a vital role in the life of Christians. The Holy Spirit encourages us, strengthens us, and fills us with all the fruits—love, patience, kindness, self-control, and so on. What are your kids missing in their lives?

Challenge your kids to ask God to take more control of their lives and to fill them with his Spirit. The closer they are to God, the more his Spirit works in them. What can they do today to get closer to God and get filled with the Spirit?

MORE

● What are the top three questions that your group has about the Holy Spirit? You may want to discuss these questions with the group and invite your senior pastor to help, too. Or have groups of your kids find one piece of information on the Holy Spirit. Encourage them to ask a parent, teacher, pastor, sibling, look through their Bible, or look on the Internet, and bring in the info next meeting.

● Or dig into the Bible to find some info! Break your group up into three groups and have each group find verses that describe each part of the Trinity—God, Jesus, and the Spirit. Compare these verses and descriptions of each part. How does the Bible describe each one? Is each part the same? What are the differences between them? Is one more powerful than another?

STRESSED OUT

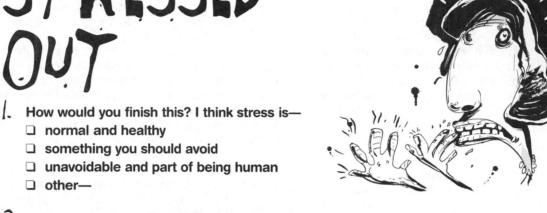

1. How would you finish this? I think stress is—
   - ❑ normal and healthy
   - ❑ something you should avoid
   - ❑ unavoidable and part of being human
   - ❑ other—

2. **Check** any of the following situations that produce
   stress in your life, and then rate how often do you deal with these situations.
   1—I deal with this a lot.   2—I deal with this sometimes.   3—I don't deal with this.

   ___ Returning home after curfew
   ___ Breaking up with your boyfriend
       or girlfriend
   ___ Losing your best friend
   ___ Studying late at night for an exam
   ___ Lying to your parents and having
       them find out
   ___ Flunking a test
   ___ Being told your parents are getting
       a divorce
   ___ Giving in to peer pressure
   ___ Applying for a job
   ___ Taking your driver's license test
   ___ Getting bad marks on your
       report card
   ___ Hearing your parents argue
       and fight

   ___ Being called on by the teacher and
       not knowing the answer
   ___ Doing something you know is wrong
   ___ Having a pet die
   ___ Being pressured to have sex
   ___ Being pressured to date
   ___ Being a victim of school violence
   ___ Going out on your first date
   ___ Arguing with your brother or sister
   ___ Being stopped by a policeman
   ___ Having no money
   ___ Moving to another town
   ___ Getting a terrible haircut
   ___ Fighting with your parents
   ___ Other—

3. Scott hasn't been doing well in his classes. He knows he's been slacking because he's
   been busy with work and baseball practices. Now his school counselor warns him that
   if his grades don't improve, he'll lose his shot at college scholarships and possibly
   admission. What would you do if you were Scott?

4. **Choose one** of the following Bible passages, and rewrite in your own words.
   Psalm 55:22   Proverbs 3:5,6
   Matthew 6:33,34   Philippians 4:6,7
   1 Peter 5:7

STRESSED OUT [s t r e s s]

THIS WEEK

Stress is a fact of life for young people and adults. Unfortunately teenagers today have more stress than ever before. Most of these stressors are put on them by parents, peers, teachers, and the church. Media tells teenagers one thing, while their parents and church tell them another. They must balance friends, schoolwork, athletics, family and fun all at the same time. This TalkSheet will help your group talk about stress and how they can handle it as Christians.

OPEN

Have your group list the stresses that youth face today. Where do they feel pressure from? Make a list of these on a whiteboard or poster board. Now for each one, how do teenagers (in general) deal with these stressors? What are good ways of dealing with stress and not so good ways? How does dealing with some stress lead to more stress?

THE DISCUSSION, BY NUMBERS

1. Let the group share their different views. Point out the fact that both answers are true at times; stress is normal and healthy (it's an internal warning to signal a problem that needs to be dealt with) and yet there are times when it should be avoided. Everyone needs a certain amount of stress-free time. Some people need more than others.

2. How do your kids feel when they face pressures? How do they handle each different situation? Don't force anyone to share their answers.

3. Use this tension-getter to lead into a discussion about the rationalization and avoidance techniques people use to avoid facing stress. What do your kids think about this situation?

4. Divide the kids into small groups, having each interpret one of these verses in regards to stress. Encourage them to be creative in their interpretations, concentrating on specific teenage problems.

THE CLOSE

Stress is normal—but too much unresolved stress can wear people down, both physically and mentally. Stress makes people sick and causes frustration and depression.

Make sure your kids understand that it's important to deal with stress, worry, or pressure. If they feel overwhelmed, to the point where they are feeling depressed or sick, they have to let it out. Challenge them to find a trusted adult who they can talk to and let the pressure out. Encourage them to

come to you with questions about stress in their lives. And if a parent or friend seems uptight, upset, or tired (and maybe takes it out on them), give the some space and encourage them. People can help each other deal with their pressures.

Encourage them to find other ways to deal with stress—to exercise, journal their feelings, play music, or read a book. Do something constructive to ease the stress and get their minds on something else. Take a study break, walk the dog, volunteer to do the dishes, or relax on the couch. Stress can be good, but don't let it make you lazy! Too much stress isn't always an excuse to get out of doing what you're supposed to do. Encourage them to ask God for patience and peace when they are feeling stressed out. Prayer is the best way to vent to God and lay situations before him.

MORE

- How do different people deal with stress? It's important to deal with substance and physical abuse. Some of your kids may have family members or friends who are abused by their parents or siblings. Stress, like anger, is never an excuse for anyone to hit or abuse anyone. Communicate that if your kids ever face an abusive situation, or know a friend who does, they must find a trusted adult immediately. Physical, sexual, and substance abuse is against the law—it's a serious crime.

- Plan a fun, de-stressing activity for and with your kids. Do something fun and spontaneous with the group. Surprise them with a dessert night, a movie night, or a trip to the beach. Make sure that everyone is welcome and included.

- When someone is stressed out, they need to be encouraged. Challenge your kids to encourage three people during the week—friends, family members, or teachers. Have them send an e-mail or letter, encouraging the person and telling them what they appreciate about them. Or draw names among your group challenge them to encourage and pray for the person who they drew.

LOOKING UP

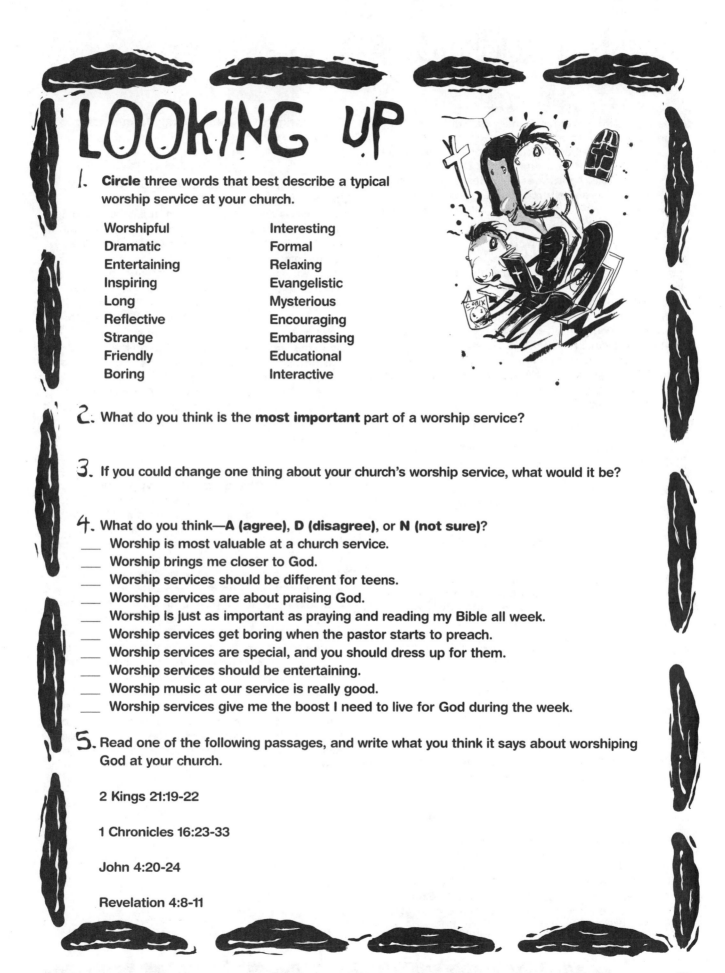

1. **Circle** three words that best describe a typical worship service at your church.

Worshipful	Interesting
Dramatic	Formal
Entertaining	Relaxing
Inspiring	Evangelistic
Long	Mysterious
Reflective	Encouraging
Strange	Embarrassing
Friendly	Educational
Boring	Interactive

2. What do you think is the **most important** part of a worship service?

3. If you could change one thing about your church's worship service, what would it be?

4. What do you think—**A (agree)**, **D (disagree)**, or **N (not sure)**?

___ Worship is most valuable at a church service.

___ Worship brings me closer to God.

___ Worship services should be different for teens.

___ Worship services are about praising God.

___ Worship Is just as important as praying and reading my Bible all week.

___ Worship services get boring when the pastor starts to preach.

___ Worship services are special, and you should dress up for them.

___ Worship services should be entertaining.

___ Worship music at our service is really good.

___ Worship services give me the boost I need to live for God during the week.

5. Read one of the following passages, and write what you think it says about worshiping God at your church.

2 Kings 21:19-22

1 Chronicles 16:23-33

John 4:20-24

Revelation 4:8-11

LOOKING UP [worship]

THIS WEEK

Some high schoolers don't understand the importance and meaning of worship. Some think it's just a boring meeting that their parents force them to attend. Others don't think it applies to them at all. This TalkSheet provides the opportunity to discuss your church worship service and to encourage your youth group to take their worship service more seriously.

OPEN

You may want to start with a role-play situation like this—

Anna keeps hearing some kids at school talk about their church services. Anna isn't a Christian and doesn't understand what they're talking about—or why they're excited about it. So she finally asks one of them what church is all about and why they go to worship services. How would your kids respond to the following questions in this circumstance?

* Why do they go to church?
* What's good (or not) about it?
* Does going to church mean that you are a Christian?
* Will your kids ask Anna to go with them sometime?
* Do they ever face situations like this at their school?

THE DISCUSSION, BY NUMBERS

1. Ask everyone to explain why they chose the words they did. Don't put down or argue any of those that are negative comments—everyone may have a different opinion.

2. Make a list of all the ingredients of a worship service and ask which they think is most important (it might be helpful to provide copies of your church's bulletin for their reference). Discuss the reasons for each different part in the order of worship.

3. What parts of the service does the group not like? Point out that some parts might indeed be boring, but this doesn't necessarily make them unacceptable or without purpose. Encourage them to take their comments or suggestions to the pastor or the church's worship committee.

4. This exercise focuses on the different aspects of worship and the service itself. Let them debate the statements that are controversial. You may want to add that there are many ways to worship God. For example, people can worship God, obey him, and do his will, but that doesn't mean they shouldn't go to church.

5. What insights have they gained from reading these Bible verses?

THE CLOSE

What are your kids' views of worship? Why is worship important? Consider these ideas—

* Worship is a verb, not a noun. It isn't something they attend in order to be entertained. Instead, it is something they do. They worship God. The worship service helps us do that.
* The worship service brings everyone in the church together, both young and old, which is important. The church is people, the community of God, and it is important for the church to have that common experience together. Corporate worship (worship with others) is one way they acknowledge the church is the body of Christ and how much they need each other.
* Worship is for God, not for us. The question to ask after a worship service is not "Did I like it?" but "Did God like it?" and "Did I do my best for him?"

MORE

● Get involved! Plan a worship service with your youth group. Let them choose the theme, pick and lead the songs, or plan and perform a skit. Give them some freedom to be creative and different. Have them meet with the senior pastor or worship leader, who can give them some direction if needed.

● And encourage your kids to get involved in different parts of the morning service, such as scripture reading, ushering, offering, greeting, and so on. They are an invaluable part of the church! You may want or need to work with your planning committee to get your youth involved in the services.

● There are several praise and worship rallies and retreats for youth of all ages. One of includes DCLA—Youth For Christ (www.yfc.org). These mass events give kids a chance to learn and worship with others their age. They often include big name Christian artists and speakers that give a new light to worship and praising the King. You can find more information on these events and links at www.YouthSpecialties.com.

THE CHOICE IS YOURS

1. List three big **life-changing decisions** that you must make in the future. When will you need to make these decisions?

2. **Rank** the following decisions from **easiest to make (1)** to **most difficult (15).**
   ___ Doing homework or going to the mall
   ___ What video or movie to watch
   ___ How to spend your free time
   ___ What kind of music to listen to
   ___ How to treat your parents when you're in trouble
   ___ What statement you make with your clothes
   ___ How often you do your personal devotions
   ___ What to do on Friday and Saturday nights
   ___ Who to go out with
   ___ What to spend money on
   ___ What Internet sites you visit
   ___ Where to draw the line with physical intimacy
   ___ What do to after high school and in the future
   ___ Who to hang out with
   ___ How to treat others

3. How would you answer these? **Y (yes), N (no)**, or **S (sometimes)**?
   ___ Do you have difficulty making up your mind?
   ___ Do you feel you have too many choices in your life?
   ___ Do you consider the consequences of your decisions before making them?
   ___ Do you often change your mind after you have made a decision?

4. What do you do—or who do you go to— when you need help making a big decision?

5. What do each of the following Bible verses say about **making decisions**?
   Proverbs 3:5-6

   Matthew 6:33

   1 Peter 5:8

THE CHOICE IS YOURS [decision making]

THIS WEEK

Young people are faced with making a multitude of decisions, but have very little decision-making experience. They need practice in making good decisions. This TalkSheet will give them an opportunity to learn about making decisions from a Christian point of view.

OPEN

Start by gift-wrapping some items in different paper. Include a variety of different items, such as soemthing valuable (gift certificate or $5 bill), invaluable (a rock or plastic cup), ugly or strange (like a white elephant gift), and so on. Announce that one package contains something that they'd like, another contains something worthless, and another has nothing in it at all. Divide them into groups to decide which they would like to have. They cannot touch the gifts before deciding. Once they've made up their minds, decide (by drawing straws, picking numbers, or flipping a coin) which group gets to choose first, second, third, and so on.

There will probably be disagreements within each group, but they have to make a decision. After the gifts have been taken, tell the group something like, "Since it was hard to pick the gift you wanted, this is a good time to talk about decision-making!"

THE DISCUSSION, BY NUMBERS

1. Ask what big decisions they anticipate making in the future and discuss them. What ones do they have in common?

2. Invite them to share their hardest decisions as well as their easiest ones. Ask why some were more difficult than others and encourage them to share the others they listed.

3. Oftentimes young people don't think about the consequences of their decisions. In a situation such as whether or not to accept drugs from a friend at a party, ask them to brainstorm the consequences as well as the benefits. Are the potential consequences worth it? Impulsive decisions that could be harmful can often be checked by remembering to ask yourself, "And then what?"

4. Who do your kids go to for help with decision making? Make a list of their suggestions, and discuss the practical how-tos of making decisions: (1) gather all the facts, (2) consider all the alternatives, (3) get some good advice, (4) pray, and (5) choose the best alternative.

5. Lead them into relating these Bible verses to practical situations. Encourage them to seek God's perspective when making decisions.

THE CLOSE

Big decisions are really a combination of little decisions. The choices they make today will set the foundation for their future. Encourage your group to start making wise decisions about little things—they'll be more confident when it is time to make important ones.

It's wise to seek good advice and think about the consequences of their decisions. How will this decision affect others around them? How will it affect their own lives? Point out that everyone makes wrong choices. That's normal and okay—the key is to learn from those mistakes. Sometimes there's no right or wrong decision. God may not have an answer for them—he'll force them to make the choice. Encourage your kids to bring their decisions before God and to ask for his wisdom. Then make a decision and move on, leaving poor decisions behind and becoming better decision makers.

Point out that God forgives—and forgets—bad choices and mistakes. That's the awesome part about God's grace and mercy. Encourage your kids to bring their past failures to God ask him to take care of their guilt and struggles in the future.

MORE

- Sometimes kids don't want to hear what adults have to say. They don't realize that parents and other adults have faced the same decisions that they do. You may want to include some other adults in this discussion, including some college, or post-college, or early adults. Present decisions (from the list above) to each one and have them share how they would decide. Give your kids the chance to ask questions about why they made the decision. Use this time to build respect for others ideas and opinions.

- How do others—non-Christian teens or adults—make decisions? Some go to horoscopes, some to Internet chat rooms, advice columns and talk shows. What other ways are there to make decisions? How would God want us to make our decisions? How can your kids rely on God for decisions—even when they can't hear his voice?

USER

1. What types of **drugs** do high schoolers use?

2. What percentage of kids at your school do you think use drugs on a regular basis? **Circle one**.

   10%   25%

   50%   75%

   Other—

3. If you could talk to a seventh-grade class about drug abuse, what would be your **three main** points?

4. What do you think—**A (agree)**, **D (disagree)**, or **U (unsure)**?

   ___ The dangers of experimenting with drugs far outweigh the benefits of trying them.

   ___ Drugs can have a positive influence on a person's life.

   ___ If a friend were to offer me drugs, I would end the friendship.

   ___ Occasional drug use will not be harmful to a young person.

   ___ I think drinking alcohol is just as bad as taking drugs.

   ___ Parents should talk regularly with their teens about drug abuse.

   ___ Street drugs should be legalized.

5. Todd has noticed a change in his friend Avery. Avery has been withdrawn and tired. He's been partying hard on the weekends and smoking weed. Avery complained yesterday that he was failing two of his classes. He hasn't been studying at all and says he can't concentrate. Todd thinks that Avery's drug habit has gone too far.

   What do you think Todd should say to Avery?

   How would you handle this situation?

   Is Todd risking the friendship to find Avery some help?

6. Check out the following Bible verses. How do they relate to substance abuse?

   Romans 12:1-2   1 Corinthians 10:31

   1 Corinthians 3:16-17   1 Corinthians 10:31

   1 Corinthians 10:13

USER [substance abuse]

THIS WEEK

America is a drugged society. Drugs are everywhere—from the medicine cabinet to the streets of our cities. Young people face tremendous pressure to experiment with drugs. They most likely know where to go for drugs and how to use them. But, they rarely talk about drugs in a Christian environment. This TalkSheet encourages an open discussion about drugs, dealing with the risks and consequences for people, including Christians.

OPEN

As you start, keep in mind that some of your kids may be using drugs, may have tried drugs, or have friends or family members who do. Be extra sensitive to your group members and be careful not to sound too judgmental.

On a whiteboard or poster board, make a list of all the different drugs your kids know of—they might be able to list quite a few. Have an additional list ready—you can find these on the Internet as well. Check out the National Institute of Drug Abuse (www.nida.nih.gov/NIDAHome1.html), the Addiction Research Foundation (www.arf.org/isd/info.html), or The National Clearinghouse for Alcohol and Drug Information (www.health.org/pubs/qdocs/). Drugs include anything that alters the body and mind, including caffeine and paint thinner—not just the hard-core street drugs. Ask, by a show of hands, how many of these drugs your kids have had exposure to. What about their friends? Do they know people who have used these drugs?

THE DISCUSSION, BY NUMBERS

1. Write down all the reasons the group listed. Choose three or four of the most common to discuss.

2. This isn't an attempt to discover who is using drugs, so don't let anyone mention names. The object is to find out to what extent drugs are being used by those in your area's high schools. Follow up with a question such as, "Would you say that drugs are easy to get on your campus?"

3. What information would they give about using drugs? You may want to have them put together what they would say to a class of seventh graders.

4. Ask for a show of hands regarding the last statement. How many have talked with their parents about drugs? You may want to role-play different parent-teen situations to make conversations with their parents easier.

5. Use this tension-getter to talk about the peer pressure to use drugs. Ask them to describe situations where they have been under pressure to try drugs.

6. Explain that the Bible doesn't specifically say, "Do not do drugs." Scripture does, however, give us guidelines and principles for making decisions about things that are harmful—like drugs. Read these passages and let several of the kids interpret them in relation to drug use.

THE CLOSE

Many young people equate having fun with drug use or drinking alcohol. Emphasize there is nothing fun about brain damage, sickness, or death—all of which can be the results of drug use. Using drugs is not only illegal, but it is deadly.

Communicate that all illegal drugs are harmful and dangerous, even those which are relatively inexpensive and available—like glue, paint, and other chemicals that some teenagers use to get high.

Ask your kids why they think people do drugs. Point out that people use drugs because their lives are empty—they believe drugs will make them happy.

Christians recognize that happiness and peace come only from following Christ. Why do people want to break God's command to take care of our bodies.

Do they consider using drugs to be sinful?

If your kids are having problems with drugs, or if they know someone who is, or if they have questions, encourage them to talk with a school counselor, parent, teacher, or you. The sooner they quit, the better. Drugs are addictive—the more they do it, the more they'll need to keep doing it.

MORE

- How familiar are your kids with doing drugs? Ask them to compile a list of terms associated with drug users. Discuss with them why there is so much drug terminology and how this influences the young people of today.

- How much do your kids know about drugs? Are they aware of the types, the names, and the effects? You may ask groups to do some research on the kinds of drugs readily available. They should find out the street names of drugs and what effect they have on the body and on behavior. You might want to have a doctor or a drug expert present some up-to-date information about drugs to your youth group.

LIVIN' IT UP

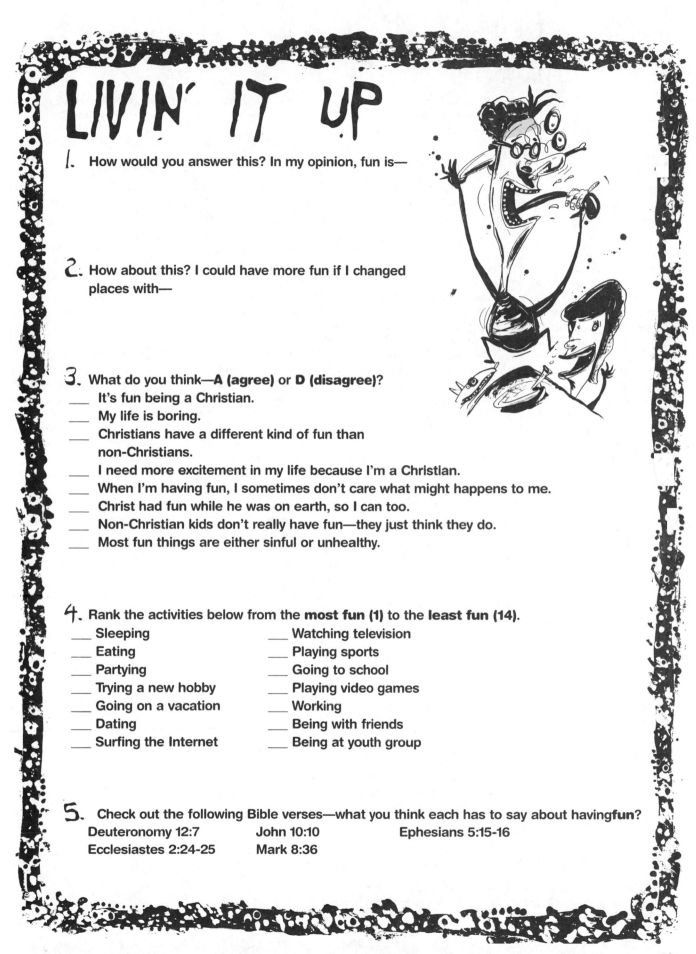

1. How would you answer this? In my opinion, fun is—

2. How about this? I could have more fun if I changed places with—

3. What do you think—**A (agree)** or **D (disagree)?**
___ It's fun being a Christian.
___ My life is boring.
___ Christians have a different kind of fun than non-Christians.
___ I need more excitement in my life because I'm a Christian.
___ When I'm having fun, I sometimes don't care what might happens to me.
___ Christ had fun while he was on earth, so I can too.
___ Non-Christian kids don't really have fun—they just think they do.
___ Most fun things are either sinful or unhealthy.

4. Rank the activities below from the **most fun (1)** to the **least fun (14)**.
___ Sleeping   ___ Watching television
___ Eating   ___ Playing sports
___ Partying   ___ Going to school
___ Trying a new hobby ___ Playing video games
___ Going on a vacation ___ Working
___ Dating   ___ Being with friends
___ Surfing the Internet ___ Being at youth group

5. Check out the following Bible verses—what you think each has to say about having **fun**?
   Deuteronomy 12:7   John 10:10   Ephesians 5:15-16
   Ecclesiastes 2:24-25 Mark 8:36

LIVIN' IT UP [h a v i n g   f u n]

THIS WEEK

Many young people don't know how to have fun. They're facing so many adult pressures and issues that many youth forget how to play. Others play too much and too hard. Youth have mistaken fun with substance abuse and other unhealthy activities. If someone acts crazy or spontaneous in a healthy way, they think he or she is high or drunk. They need to learn how to have fun creatively and safely. This TalkSheet will help you talk about having fun.

OPEN

This is your chance to make this discussion fun! Choose a few fun games and let the group play them. There are several store bought games like Outburst or Scattegories that are great for large groups. You could also check out the Ideas Library books (Youth Specialties)—there are several books of games and crowd-breakers. Or have your kids bring in their favorite music or video (but be sure you screen what is shown or played!). You may also want to have your kids or parents bring in a variety of fun food—pizza, soda, chips, cookies, or ice cream sundaes.

Or you may want to plan a random fun event, such as a scavenger hunt or another activity that you normally wouldn't do at a typical meeting.

THE DISCUSSION, BY NUMBERS

1. Make a master list of all their definitions of fun—both positive and negative answers. Why did they choose these answers? Keep the list in view in case you want to refer to it.

2. Ask the kids to explain why they chose the person they named. Don't ask for specific names, but ask them why they want to be that person? What does he or she have that they don't have?

3. Read the statements aloud and ask for volunteers to express their opinion. Ask that they explain their answers. For example, some might disagree to the statement it is fun being a Christian.
Some of the statements explore the need for constant excitement. Young people who are always living on the edge are headed for trouble.
Partying has become a major sport. Fun is healthy and good, but destructive fun can be potentially dangerous.
Ask the members of your group why they think so many young people choose to have fun in harmful ways, such as substance abuse.

4. Ask them to share their choices for most fun and least fun. What are healthy ways of having fun? Why do some teens equate fun with recklessness? Discuss some of these issues with your group.

5. Read the Bible verses outloud and ask the group what the verses say about having fun. Try dividing the kids into smaller groups for this part of the discussion.

THE CLOSE

God does want us to have fun! He isn't a cosmic killjoy—or a corrective parent—sitting up in heaven with a frown on his face. He wants us to enjoy life at its fullest—that's why he created all the things they enjoy. He's the creator of life, he knows what's best for us, and how we can get the most out of life. Read Philippians 4:4 where Paul encourages us to rejoice.

It is possible to have fun without getting into trouble. Your kids will probably encounter many situations as they grow older when they'll face decisions about drugs and alcohol. Emphasize that having fun is not synonymous with getting wasted. Losing control, getting sick, and risking irreversible brain damage is not fun. Encourage your kids to pursue activities without doing anything they'll regret later.

MORE

- Plan a big fun event with your kids during a weekend or school break. This could include a special event, a trip to an amusement park, or an overnight camping trip. Let your budget and your creativity guide you. You may want to have a special fundraiser with your group to raise money for this. Then go and have a rockin' time with your kids!

- Have your kids do some research on fun things to do in the area. This is more difficult if you live in a small town! Have them check out the Internet for information on events or things going on in your area. Or on a whiteboard or poster board, brainstorm together fun activities that they could do. Challenge them to think creatively (not just renting movies), but to think of ways that they can spice up their fun times, even if it is low key.

SO NOBODY'S PERFECT

1. What do you think **sin** is?

2. List **three sins** that some high schoolers consider okay.

3. What do you think—**T (true)** or **F (false)**?
   ___ Some sins are worse than others.
   ___ What was a sin 10 years ago may not be a sin today.
   ___ Christians don't intentionally sin.
   ___ If a sin doesn't hurt anyone, it's not really a sin.
   ___ Since God forgives our sins, they really aren't that big of a deal.
   ___ One way or another, we will always pay for our sins.
   ___ God forgets all of our sins when we are forgiven.

4. When you know something is wrong, but you do it anyway, how do you feel? Does it depend on the circumstances?

5. The following verses say something about sin. Check out each verse and rewrite the point in your own words.
   Psalm 1:1-3
   Psalm 130
   Proverbs 28:13
   Isaiah 55:6-7
   1 John 1:8-9

SO NOBODY'S PERFECT [s i n]

THIS WEEK

What is sin? It's a major part of the human condition and hard concept for some teenagers to understand—especially if the aren't familiar with the Bible. This TalkSheet will help explain what sin is and open a discussion about sin and what Christians can do about it.

OPEN

Since it's hard for some to understand sin (besides doing something wrong), ask your group to answer the following questions. What does sin look like (in your imagination)? How would you describe sin? What causes you to sin? How much sin is too much?

They'll probably have a bunch of different answers. Take some time to make a master list of these answers. Why did they pick the answers they did? What helps them understand sin better?

Is your group too antsy to talk through these questions? Collect and pass out newspapers or magazines to the kids and ask them to find a few examples of sin. Go around and have them share one or two examples that they found. What was the sin? Why is it considered a sin? How would the sin rate on a scale of 1-10?

THE DISCUSSION, BY NUMBERS

1. Try to reach a consensus for a definition of sin with your group. Point out that sin is more than specific misdoings, it's a rebellion against God and his laws.

2. The kids will probably include things like getting drunk, having illicit sex, cheating on exams, telling white lies, and so on. Make a master list of the group's answers. Talk about why these are sometimes considered permissible. Discuss the main ones that are mentioned and ask why they believe them to be sinful.

3. As they share their responses to these statements, encourage them to think of biblical support for their opinions. You might want to divide them into the true and false sections. Have them consult a Bible concordance or a topical Bible for supporting their point of view. Help your kids understand that God loves them and that he does forgive them, but sin hurts God. Their sinfulness sent Jesus to the cross—no one can make light of their sins.

   The Bible says that, "You may be sure that your sin will find you out" (Numbers 32:23). Sin would have few takers if its consequences happened immediately. The main reason God doesn't want us to sin is because sin is destructive to us. Not only are we disobeying God when we sin, but

we're hurting ourselves as well as God. Even seemingly little sins can cause problems. Although God forgives us our sins, we may have to deal with their consequences for a long time. The point here isn't to frighten the kids or to ladle guilt, but to let them know the dangers of sin.

4. How did your kids respond to this question? What situations would make sinning worse (such as speeding in a car vs. cheating on an exam)? You may want to refer to the verses in question 5.

5. Read these Bible passages aloud with the group. They are intended to move the discussion from sin to grace—focus on God's forgiveness.

THE CLOSE

Everyone—parents, pastors, teachers, and friends—sins. It's a fact. They are all human and they all fall short of the glory of God. Sin distances us from God, but fortunately never separates us completely from his love. God is faithful and forgives us our sins (1 John 1:9). They get a fresh start whenever they ask for God's forgiveness.

Is there one or two sins that each group member is struggling with or feeling guilty about? You may want to ask group members to write down their sins on a piece of paper. Then demonstrate God's refining fire—his forgiveness—by burning the papers in a fire outside (just be careful!). Or (the safer option) have your kids rip them into tiny pieces. Either activity shows what Christ does with our sins—forgives and forgets. Tell the kids that they've asked for and received forgiveness from Christ. You may want to give them a moment of silent prayer or reflection time. And, remind them that they need to forgive themselves, too. They've given the sin and the guilt to God—the sin is no more.

MORE

● The Bible is chock full of examples of God's grace and forgiveness. There are several examples in the miracles and life of Christ, who showed love and mercy to sinners. In fact, Jesus hung out with unclean sinners (like Mary, a former prostitute). Have the group find some of these examples and list them on a whiteboard or poster board. Then point out that God has always and will always forgive those who love him.

● Discuss with your group the importance of forgiving others like God forgives them. What makes it hard to forgive and forget with your friends or family? How can they deal with these sins and get over the hurt caused by others? Challenge your kids to confront and forgive one person this week.

PEOPLE PLEASER

1. Place an **X** on the line below that describes where you see yourself. Are you a follower or a leader?

◆ ▌▌▌▌▌▌▌▌▌▌▌▌▌▌▌▌▌▌▌▌▌▌▌▌ ◆

Follower   Leader

2. When someone is **pressuring** you to do something you don't want to do, what do you do?
   - ❑ Lie and make up an excuse
   - ❑ Tell them it's wrong and that you won't do it
   - ❑ Simply say no
   - ❑ Go along with it anyway
   - ❑ Suggest another activity
   - ❑ Leave the room or situation
   - ❑ Other—

3. What advice would you give in each of the following situations?
   a. Tyrel's friends always pressure him to do things he knows are wrong.
   b. Santos has a hard time being himself around his friends.
   c. Julie always waits to hear her friends' opinions before giving hers.
   d. Louisa is really uncomfortable if she isn't dressed just like her friends.

4. How often do you do the following? Rate each on a scale of **1 (always)** to **6 (never)**.
   ___ I feel pressured to do what others are doing in order to be accepted.
   ___ I ask my parents for advice more often than I ask my friends.
   ___ I find it easier to speak up for what I believe, rather than to go along with the crowd.
   ___ I set my own standards, rather than live by the standards of others.
   ___ I quickly change my opinion if someone tries to argue with me.
   ___ I find that it's difficult to live a Christian life around my friends.

5. Check out these verses, and complete the sentences in your own words.
Romans 12:1-2	If I try to conform to other people at school—
1 Corinthians 15:33	I spend my time with people who—
Hebrews 11:24-26	I have chosen to be like—

PEOPLE PLEASER [p e e r   p r e s s u r e]

THIS WEEK

Here's the reality—peer pressure surrounds our teenagers. They spend less time with their families, attend classes with large groups of peers, work at jobs with people their age, play sports with friends, and talk on the phone with them. Teenagers learn from, grow with, and are influenced by others their age. This TalkSheet will help you to deal with the real issues facing your kids and the discuss the influences of peer pressure.

OPEN

Announce you are going to conduct a taste test, like those they've seen on TV. Have them taste two different brands of soda (like Coke and Pepsi) or ice cream (or whatever else you'd like), to determine which is best, brand A or brand B.

Beforehand, tell some of your kids to choose brand A. Their job is to persuade the others to pick the same brand. Tell them to do whatever they can to get the rest of the group to pick brand A. You'll find that some in the group will give in to this pressure and will choose brand A. Keep a tally of the results and then discuss the results. How were the kids influenced by others? Why did they listen to their peers?

Some kids won't be persuaded—congratulate them for having resisted. What made them stick up for their choice? How did they feel when the others were pressuring them? What other feelings or ideas did they have?

THE DISCUSSION, BY NUMBERS

1. Discuss the difference between being a leader and being a follower. Ask the kids to brainstorm the characteristics of each. Point out there is nothing wrong with being a follower—without followers there would be no leaders—but the trick is to make certain those you are following know where they are going, and are headed in the right direction.

2. Ask the kids to share their choices and discuss other alternatives to negative peer pressure.

3. These true-to-life situations will provide practice in dealing with similar ones in their own lives. Let them share advice and responses with each other.

4. Discuss these statements in a general way, but be careful not to embarrass anyone. Each deals with a specific aspect of peer pressure and will help kids evaluate their own vulnerability. Choose one or two to emphasize, such as the one regarding parents. Try to help them stretch their minds and think through the consequences of giving in.

5. Allow kids to share their completed sentences and thoughts on these verses. Do they think God understands peer pressure? Why or why not?

THE CLOSE

There's nothing wrong with going along with friends—as long as it isn't illegal, unethical, harmful, or likewise. God has given people beliefs and a conscience. He trusts that they'll respect themselves and him enough to make wise choices. Real friends respect each other's opinions and beliefs.

There's no doubt that the values of the world are going to be in opposition to the values of the kingdom of God. Your kids need to seek first the kingdom of God (Matthew 6:33) to help them consistently make the right decision.

Point out that Christ also was tempted in all things—just as all people are—and he understands. Christ can help in their struggles and the power of the Holy Spirit will enable them to be self-controlled—a fruit of the Spirit—rather than be crowd-controlled.

MORE

● Ask your group to find examples in the media of how kids influence other kids. They'll find examples of this pressure (anything from stealing to having sex) on nearly every teenage TV show and in magazine advertisements. Have them bring a few examples of this pressure and discuss if the media portrays peer pressure as good or bad.

● Do your kids have a solid list of their personal beliefs and values? Have them make a list of their beliefs and values—then sign the list as a contract for themselves as things they won't compromise on (such as doing drugs or having premarital sex). Encourage them to set personal goals for themselves and to include God in this goal. No temptation is too great to resist with God on their side.

LIAR, LIAR

1. Rank the following from the **most dishonest (1)** to the **least dishonest (10)**.
   ___ Lying to parents so you can go out with friends
   ___ Plagiarizing information off the Internet for your term paper
   ___ Shoplifting a gift for someone
   ___ Giving an untrue excuse to a teacher
   ___ Protecting a friend by lying
   ___ Goofing off when you are being paid to work
   ___ Giving false information about yourself in an on-line chat room
   ___ Cheating on your test
   ___ Telling your girlfriend or boyfriend you couldn't call because the phone was broken
   ___ Making illegal copies of a video or CD

2. What do you think—**Y (yes)** or **N (no)**?
   ___ A student can get through school without lying.
   ___ The truth should always be told, no matter what the consequences are.
   ___ If we want to make it to the top, we'll have to be a little dishonest at times.
   ___ People can't be true friends if they are not honest with each other.
   ___ There are times when it's impossible to be honest with parents.
   ___ Lying can sometimes be an act of kindness.
   ___ Lying is permissible as long as it doesn't hurt anyone and we don't get caught.
   ___ It's acceptable to tell an occasional white lie.

3. What would you do in the following situations?
   a. A friend is spreading an untrue rumor about a person you know.

   b. You find a watch in the locker room—you need a watch!

   c. A good friend has a new haircut that you think is ugly—and she asks if you like it.

   d. Your mom asks you to help her out—you want to go out with your friends.

   e. You've cheated on your boyfriend without him knowing.

4. Below (or on the back of this sheet) summarize **Psalm 15** in your own words.

LIAR, LIAR [h o n e s t y]

THIS WEEK

It's easy to get away with being dishonest these days. One can easily "fake it" in an on-line chat room, shoplift small items at the store, or fib to their parents. But dishonesty is more than just telling lies. How do your high schoolers view honesty versus a value? They must decide whether or not to be a completely honest person. This TalkSheet discusses honesty and why God is an advocate of it!

OPEN

How well does your group know each other? Try playing Two Truths and a Lie. Have the kids write three statements about themselves, two that are true and one that is not. If the kids choose two truths that sound like lies and a lie that sounds true, they'll be able to fool the group. The group must try to guess which one of the three is a lie.

Another idea is to conduct a lying contest. Have a contest to find out who can tell the biggest lie. After each student has told his fib, vote on the best tall tale. Give a prize to the winner, or simply announce you'll give $10 to the winner—then later admit that you lied!

THE DISCUSSION, BY NUMBERS

1. Ask for some volunteers to reveal their choices and give reasons. Expect considerable disagreement and encourage debating about the different answers. Why would some qualify as worse than others?

2. There may be some difficulty with this exercise because the answers must be either yes or no. Divide them according to their answers and allow them to debate issues.

3. These tension-getters offer some true-to-life situations to bring up for discussion. Allow them to share what they would actually do. Keep the general attitude open and free from put-downs, or they will be inclined to lie about their answers and merely tell you what they think you want to hear.

4. Ask them to read their paraphrases. In addition to Psalm 15, you may ask them to search the Bible verses for more passages related to honesty.

THE CLOSE

You may want to focus some of your closing remarks on the consequences of honesty and dishonesty. How can dishonesty can blow up in your face? Help your group understand that one lie tends to lead to another. And being known as a dishonest person can ruin your reputation and your sense of self-worth. One of the key characteristics of a Christian is honesty and being trustworthy. How can your kids imitate Christ? By being truthful and honest as he was. Remind them that God will forgive and forget them for past lies.

MORE

● While they are watching TV, listening to the radio, reading magazines, and surfing the Internet this week, have your kids look for dishonesty in the media. How does the media use dishonesty to sell products, make money, or lie to the public? In what ways is the media dishonest? Are there specific TV shows, advertised brands, or Web sites that are not credible?

● Challenge your kids to ask their parents for a story of when they weren't completely truthful as teenagers, and what happened as a result. Parents often have some funny (or not so funny) stories to share. Have your kids get one honesty tip from their parents to bring next time and compile those for all to see.

DO-SOMETHING@WORLD.NET

1. If you could do **one thing** to make the world a better place, what would it be?

2. The following issues are often the focus of concern for Christians. Choose **five** you consider **most significant** for believers and then number them **one (1)** to **five (5)**, in order of importance.

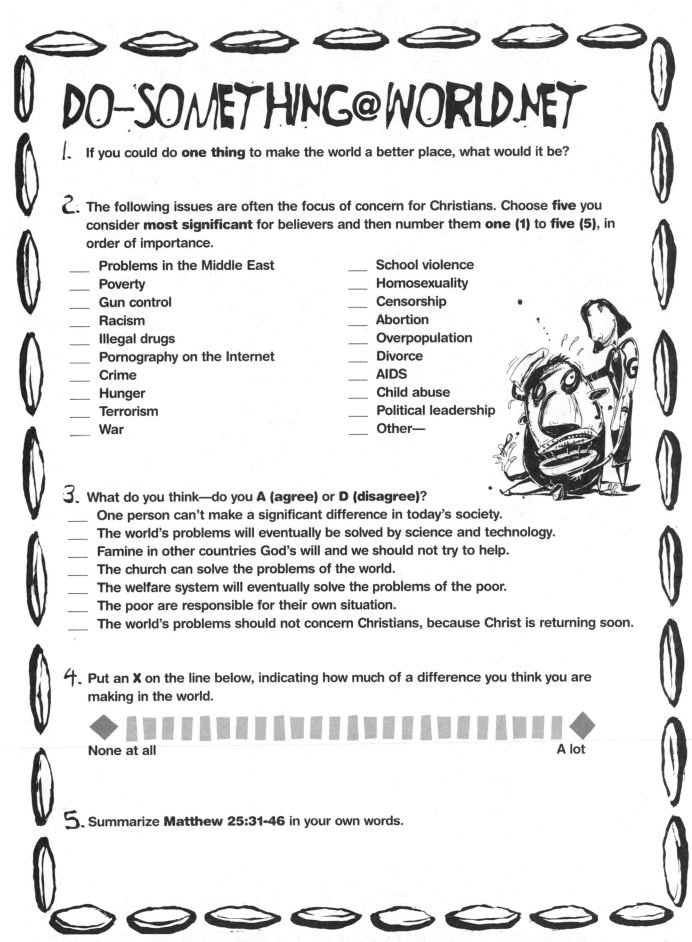

___ Problems in the Middle East
___ Poverty
___ Gun control
___ Racism
___ Illegal drugs
___ Pornography on the Internet
___ Crime
___ Hunger
___ Terrorism
___ War

___ School violence
___ Homosexuality
___ Censorship
___ Abortion
___ Overpopulation
___ Divorce
___ AIDS
___ Child abuse
___ Political leadership
___ Other—

3. What do you think—do you **A (agree)** or **D (disagree)**?
___ One person can't make a significant difference in today's society.
___ The world's problems will eventually be solved by science and technology.
___ Famine in other countries God's will and we should not try to help.
___ The church can solve the problems of the world.
___ The welfare system will eventually solve the problems of the poor.
___ The poor are responsible for their own situation.
___ The world's problems should not concern Christians, because Christ is returning soon.

4. Put an **X** on the line below, indicating how much of a difference you think you are making in the world.

None at all   A lot

5. Summarize **Matthew 25:31-46** in your own words.

DO-SOMETHING@WORLD.NET [Christian social action]

THIS WEEK

There are an overwhelming number of problems in the world—everything from poverty to social injustice. High school kids are able to give a lot, but many don't get encouraged to get into action. This TalkSheet allows you to discuss how your kids can make a difference in the world by helping others who are less fortunate.

OPEN

Are your kids up-to-date with what's going on in the world? You may want to distribute newspapers and news magazines (such as *Time* and *Newsweek*) and have groups find as many stories as possible about needy people and world problems. Allow five to ten minutes for the search. Then, have them share the stories. It may be helpful to have a world map there for them to see where the problem is going on. You may want to put stickers or marks on the places where the problems are taking place—both international or in the U.S.

What are the needs of others in the world? Role-play and discuss some situations of those in need—having no fresh water, eating only rice once every-other day, battling a disease without funds to get money, not being able to worship freely. How would your kids feel in these situations? How would their priorities be different? Would these situations change their understanding of God?

THE DISCUSSION, BY NUMBERS

1. Some of your kids may have difficulty answering this question. They need to understand that they *can* effect change in today's world! Discuss what answers they gave and how they would change the world.

2. Compare what each has listed and try to compose a master list of ten. What do they think the church can do about any of the problems? What problems are more important than others?

3. Each of these questions has the potential for further discussion. If there is disagreement on any, stop and discuss it. Point out that they can make a difference in spite of the overwhelming immensity of our world's problems. How can the little things make a difference?

4. This exercise illustrates the difference between what they are doing now and what they would like to be doing. Ask for suggestions about how they would actually go about making the world a better place. List the ideas where everyone can see.

5. Ask for a few to read their summaries and describe one thing they learned from this passage. What would Jesus say about social action?

THE CLOSE

God has given everyone gifts and abilities to help those in need—whether it be big or small. He can use each person in the room to make a difference in the world. Look at Mark 6:39-55 for example—he fed five thousand people from one small lunch! In the same way, God can and will take whatever your kids have to offer him and bless it. Because God sees and knows all things, even their somewhat small efforts will play a big role.

MORE

● Prayer is one way that your kids can help those in need. You may want to make a list of all the problems that were discussed in the introduction. Then pass this list out and ask your kids to pray for one world problem each day. Encourage them to keep an eye out for world news and keep it in their prayers. For the latest world news, check out a news Web site such as www.cnn.com or www.nbc.com.

● As a group, sponsor a needy child through an Christian organization. There are several organizations, including World Vision (www.wvi.org) or Compassion International (www.ci.org). By doing small fundraisers and/or pooling money, your group will be able to help a child in need and experience first-hand how to support someone in need.

● Dare your kids to get out there and do something! With your group, plan a service project or outreach to help those in need. A useful resource for planning is the *Ideas Library: Camps, Retreats, Missions & Service Ideas* (Youth Specialties).

ONE IS THE LONELIEST NUMBER

1. List **five words** that describe loneliness.

2. How would you answer this? I feel most lonely when—

3. Natasha hung out on Friday night with three of her friends. She likes them and had fun—but she doesn't think she fits in that well. As she journaled that night, she wrote about how lonely she felt. **Why** do you think Natasha felt lonely?

   What can she do about feeling lonely?

4. What do you think—**A (agree)** or **D (disagree)**?
   ___ Everyone gets lonely sometimes.
   ___ If someone is with other people, he or she won't be lonely.
   ___ If a person feels lonely, it's that person's fault.
   ___ If life were more exciting, young people wouldn't be lonely.
   ___ Jesus Christ felt lonely.
   ___ If you feel lonely when you're young, you'll be lonely for the rest of your life.
   ___ Adults get lonely more often than teenagers.

5. What do you **usually** do when you are lonely?

6. Read **2 Timothy 4:16-18**, and answer the questions below.
   What do you think Paul felt?

   Why do other people not always support us?

   How do you think the Lord supported Paul?

ONE IS THE LONELIEST NUMBER [loneliness]

THIS WEEK

Young people hear that the teenage years are the best years of their lives. But these years can be very lonely, even in the midst of the carefree fun. This TalkSheet offers your group the chance to talk about their lonely feelings, the causes and cures of loneliness, and how God can help.

OPEN

Before this session, you may want to ask your kids find examples or stories of loneliness—song lyrics, video clips, poems, stories from a magazine or book, and so on. Then read, play, or show these examples in the group. What message did each one give about loneliness? What words or characteristics about loneliness come to mind from each example? How was the person or artist feeling and why? How did he or she get over the loneliness, if at all? You may want to make a master list of these characteristics to refer to later.

THE DISCUSSION, BY NUMBERS

1. Make a master list of all the words chosen. What word was most commonly chosen?

2. When do your kids feel most lonely? Why or why not?

3. This tension-getter will invite discussion about the difference between loneliness and being alone. Loneliness is usually a feeling inside one-self, perhaps of being misunderstood or unappreciated. There may be feelings of inferiority causing one to feel lonely, even when surrounded by people. Take some time to talk about loneliness in this context.

4. Discuss each of these statements with your group. Allow them to express their thoughts on each one. Take the time to discuss any disagreements. Tell them Christ also felt lonely (see Matthew 13:53-57; Mark 14:22,27,31,50; 15:1-34; and Luke 4:24-30).

5. Talk with your group about ways to cure loneliness. What do your kids do when they are lonely? How do people handle loneliness in different ways? Is that good or not so good?

6. Describe how Paul faced his loneliness. Ask your group if God can do the same for them as he did for Paul. You might also want to read Psalm 146.

THE CLOSE

God created us to be in close relationships with other people. They were created to live in families and in community with others. That's why it's important for us to build friendships and protect our relationships.

Christ experienced loneliness. You may want to read a few verses that show Christ being alone. He understands every emotion and every need. Your kids may feel lonely, but they aren't ever alone. Who can they turn to when they feel down? Encourage them to find one person who they know will encourage them—including you, their teacher, school counselor, or other adult.

MORE

● How do your kids handle alone time? Challenge them to spend a half hour (or more) of their time alone, away from everyone—no TV, Internet, radio, or any other distraction. Have them concentrate on being alone with themselves, just sitting, thinking, or praying. What was hard about being alone? What did they do to keep themselves occupied?

● You may want take time and talk about loneliness versus depression. There is an alarming rate of depression among Americans, including young people. Some of your kids may deal with depression—either with themselves, with a parent, or a sibling. Loneliness and depression are not the same thing. Make sure that your kids know the difference between being lonely and depression. Constant loneliness leads to depression, depression leads to withdrawal and further loneliness. Depression, although it varies person to person, is a chronic, emotional disorder with symptoms of mood swings and suicidal thoughts. For more information and links, check out www.depression.com or www.depression.about.com/health/depression/.

SHOW ME LOVE

1. Write a statement describing–

   How do you think the world sees love?

   How do you think Christians see love?

2. Which of the following people are **easy (E)** to love? Which are **difficult (D)**?

   ___ Your mother
   ___ Your close friend
   ___ A famous singer
   ___ Yourself
   ___ Your siblings
   ___ A person of
       another race

   ___ A teacher
   ___ Your father
   ___ Your boyfriend or
       girlfriend
   ___ God
   ___ Your grandparents

   ___ A good-looking person
   ___ Your boss
   ___ A poor person
   ___ A rich person

3. Check which of the following **aren't** examples of love?
   ❏ Getting on your sister's case for doing something wrong
   ❏ Putting limits on physical intimacy
   ❏ Making a joke out of someone's mistake
   ❏ Giving money to a ministry
   ❏ Being polite to the police officer who pulls you over
   ❏ Having sex with someone
   ❏ Giving your unpopular neighbor a ride to school
   ❏ Ditching your shift at work
   ❏ Refusing to lie to cover up for a friend
   ❏ Agreeing to tutor your brother in Algebra
   ❏ Volunteering your time for the canned food drive at church
   ❏ Breaking your curfew
   ❏ Visiting questionable Web sites on the Internet
   ❏ Doing your share of chores at home

4. Check out **1 Corinthians 13:1-13**. These verses give God's description of love. Write down each characteristic of love in your own words. Use the back of this paper if you need more room.

SHOW ME LOVE [Christian love]

THIS WEEK

There are different ideas about love among teens. Some think it's a kind of gushy, sentimental emotion you have toward someone. Others think it's a physical act, seen on TV and in movies. Yet others hear that it's an action, not an emotion. Our culture and media is saturated with different ideas of love, many of which are untrue and unhealthy. With the rise in divorce rates, most kids today don't understand what love is. This TalkSheet will help you find out what your kids think about love. It teaches what love is and explains practical ways that your youth can put love into action.

OPEN

Romantic love is the hot issue in all kinds of music—from rap to swing music to country ballads. Begin this session by listening to a popular song or by watching a music video that deals with love. You can download and play songs from the Internet—check out www.mp3.com.

Or start by writing the word love on a large sheet of poster board or whiteboard. Then have your kids list words that describe love—what they think love is and how the media portrays love. You can use this list later to wrap things up.

THE DISCUSSION, BY NUMBERS

1. Compare the different statements and try to arrive at a consensus of opinion on the difference between the worldly view of love and Christian love.

2. Ask the kids to share the reasons for their answers. Why are some easier to love than others?

3. Some of these items aren't examples of love and some are. Ask your groups which statements they chose that were not examples of love. Go through each item with your kids and discuss how (or how not) each item shows love. Answer any questions they may have and leave room for them to debate any disagreements they may have. Be sure to point out that some of these are examples of not only loving others, but also loving ones self, too! God commands that we are to love our neighbors as we love ourselves (Luke 10:27). If your kids don't love themselves, there's something missing!

4. How did your kids phrase the characteristics of love in these verses? What other words or actions can describe love, based on these verses? You may want to write a group paraphrase of these verses.

THE CLOSE

In your close, be sure to point out that love is not a feeling or an emotion, but is a decision people make. The Bible doesn't ask them to like their neighbors—it commands them to love even those people they don't like.

Challenge your kids to look at people the way Christ did. Every person is a child of God, created in the image of God, and who Christ died for. Today's culture teaches people to use people and love material things—Christ teaches them to simply love others.

Close up by reflecting on the initial list of words that describe love. Discuss how the world portrays love and how Christianity portrays love. What major differences are there? How have people messed up the meaning of love? What would God have to say to our society about love?

MORE

● Who is that one person that each of your kids has a hard time loving? You may want to point out that a good way to show love to them is to pray for them. Prayer strengthens relationships—and makes them right with God. Encourage your group to do something for that person during the week—pray for them, go out of their way to say hello, or send that person and e-mail or anonymous note. What was hard about showing love to that person? How did their perspective toward that person change?

● Dig deeper into the Bible and split your group up into teams. Ask each group to find two or more verses that describe or deal with love. What do these verses say about God's love and the world's view of love?

WISE UP

1. Who is the **wisest** person you know?

2. What is the best **advice** anyone ever gave you?

3. How would you complete this statement?
   I would be much wiser if I—

4. Check **three areas** below where you could use more wisdom.
   - ❑ Staying out of trouble
   - ❑ School work and studying
   - ❑ Family life
   - ❑ Handling my emotions
   - ❑ Relationships and sex
   - ❑ Understanding the Bible
   - ❑ Choosing friends
   - ❑ Spending money
   - ❑ Listening to advice
   - ❑ Deciding about my future
   - ❑ Relating to God
   - ❑ Other—

5. What advice would you give to the parent who wrote this e-mail?
   I have three children—two teenage daughters and one teenage son. My problem is that none of them will listen to my advice. They think they know it all and that I know nothing—especially my son, the oldest. I'm concerned for their futures and want to share some of my hard-earned wisdom. I don't want them to make the same mistakes I made or those I have seen others make. What can I do?

6. Pick a chapter in the book of **Proverbs** to read and write **five pieces** of advice given in the chapter.

WISE UP [w i s d o m]

THIS WEEK

Youth hear advice from friends, teachers, parents, and the media—just to name a few sources. Who do they listen to? What will they believe? How are they able to sort out all these ideas and information? This TalkSheet is created to discuss the need for guidance and ends with a discussion on God's Word as the ultimate source of wisdom.

OPEN

Before this activity, you'll need something to write on (a newspring, poster board, or whiteboard), something to write with, and a few other items—horoscopes, some large dice, a deck of cards, a Magic 8-ball, "cootie catcher" (ask a junior high girl), advice-column clip (check a newspaper or teen magazine), a Bible and so on. Start by asking your kids to name the problems they face daily and list them on the whiteboard or poster board. (For example, what to eat for breakfast, what to wear, who to eat lunch with, or how to study for a test). Then split your group into smaller groups and give each a few of the problems listed. Their mission is to solve or answer these problems by using a "tool of wisdom"—on of the "other items" you brought with you—as their only way to make a decision or figure out their dilemmas. Then debrief the group on these sources of wisdom and how helpful (or unhelpful) they were.

THE DISCUSSION, BY NUMBERS

1. Who do your kids consider to be wise? Why? What characteristics of this person makes them wise?

2. Ask for volunteers to share their bits of good advice. Who did they hear them from? How has it helped them?

3. Let some of the kids read their completed sentences and state their reasons. Close by making the point that everyone should seek more wisdom each day.

4. After listening to their answers, point out that being wise doesn't necessarily mean being smart. Learning is one thing, but it's what you do with your learning that leads to wisdom. How can your kids gain wisdom in these areas?

5. This e-mail deals with a problem common to parents of teenagers—the know-it-all son or daughter. As the kids share their advice, try to help them see the parent's point of view, rather than just their own.

6. This exercise is appropriate for several small groups. Make sure that each takes a different chapter. Allow sufficient time for them to think of five statements of wise advice. The purpose is learning to use the Bible as a source of wisdom for daily living. Encourage them to look at God's Word for help in practical ways.

THE CLOSE

Discuss with your kids how to seek God's wisdom through prayer, Bible study, and the advice from other Christians. Warn the group to be aware of the advice that they get from their friends, the media, and other outside sources—it's easy to hear the wrong message and make the wrong choices. God has given them the ability to discern and evaluate what is going on. And, remind them that "the fear of the Lord is the beginning of knowledge" (Proverbs 1:7)—true wisdom comes from God. The more they love God and keep his commandments, the more wisdom they'll receive.

MORE

- With the group, write down five issues that young people want advice on—choosing friends, dating, dealing with anger, doing drugs, and so on. You may want to have them look for Bible verses that deal with these issues. It may be helpful to use a topical Bible or search an on-line Bible for passages. Have them look through Proverbs as well—Solomon was a smart guy. Then discuss these verses and how they apply. What does God have to say about this?

- Q & A time—you may want to use a panel of adult parents or a combination of adults and kids. Have your kids write questions that they want advice on (make sure these aren't signed). Put these in a box and read them one at a time. Then, have the adults give their advice or opinion on the situation. This is a great way for kids to interact with adults and hear perspectives from other people, not just you or their peers.

- Where do people look for advice in today's society? A few examples include advice columns in newspapers and magazines (such as "Dear Abby"), question and answer columns in teen magazines (such as *Teen* or *Seventeen*), radio or TV shows such as Dr. Laura or Oprah, and self-help books. Which of these have your kids gone to for advice? Which sources are most reliable or give the most honest advice? Why or why not? Take some time to talk about these trends in a society that is seeking wisdom.

CHANNEL SURFIN'

1. List three **positive** and three **negative** things about television.

2. **Circle** an answer for each of the following.
Why do you watch TV?
Because there's nothing better to do.
Because it's entertaining and fun.
Because it's educational.
Other—

What would you do if a friend called during your favorite show?
❑ Return the call later, after the program.
❑ Talk on the telephone while watching the program.
❑ Turn the set off and talk to my friend.
❑ Other—

What would you do if your TV broke?
❑ Try to talk my parents into buying another one immediately.
❑ Find something else to do, to occupy my time.
❑ Have a huge withdrawal.
❑ Other—

3. Are the following statements true for you **all of the time (A), some of the time (S),** or **never (N)?**
___ i watch over 20 hours of TV per week.
___ I watch TV even though I should be doing something else, like homework.
___ I'm influenced by commercials.
___ I'm conscious of my TV watching time.
___ I watch shows that contain a lot of sex and violence.
___ I watch music videos.
___ I turn on the TV as soon as I walk in the door.
___ I study with the TV on.

4. Decide which of the following Bible verses apply to TV and how?

Exodus 20:3-61   Corinthians 10:31   Joshua 14:1-2   Galatians 2:1

CHANNEL SURFIN' [t e l e v i s i o n]

THIS WEEK

Television, the tube, the telly (to use British slang), the TV. Call it what you will, but the TV rules the American household. The average person watches hours of television every week. There is a TV station for nearly everyone with any interest—from sports lovers to rap music fans. Most homes have more than one television and most young children can name cartoon characters. The TV is the life of U.S. culture—telling people what they need or don't need, what they should eat, drink, or where, and how they should look, act, and behave.

This TalkSheet raises important questions for Christians. You can't tell your kids to turn the TV off all together, but you can teach them good viewing skills. The purpose of this session is to talk about TV and teach them how to evaluate what they watch.

OPEN

On a large piece of newsprint or whiteboard, draw a blank television schedule for the week, writing only the days, certain channels, and certain evening times (such as Fox Network, Monday, 7:00 p.m. or NBC, Tuesday, 8:00 p.m.). Then ask the kids to guess or tell you what shows air at those specific times. You'll be surprised how much they know! Have the correct answers available in order to check their responses. For information on show times in your area check out Gist TV (www.gist.com/tv/) or www.askjeves.com then type in the keywords "television shows.'

Want to take it further? Ask your group to rank the shows as good, bad, or questionable on a scale of 1-10, with stars, or however you want to. Talk about the different kinds of shows and what age group(s) they think each show is meant for. Then, discuss how each show portrays people of different ages—especially teenagers, parents, and religion.

THE DISCUSSION, BY NUMBERS

1. Discuss the positives and negatives that your group wrote down and make a master list of them on a poster board or whiteboard. Does everyone agree with these points? Why or why not? Why do some people think the TV has different positives and negatives?

2. How did your kids respond to these questions? What other answers did they give? Point out that their answers may show them just how much TV rules their lives! How can they begin to make changes in their viewing habits?

3. This activity will help the kids evaluate their viewing habits. Don't force them to reveal their answers, but talk about each of the statements in general terms. Did they have trouble being honest with themselves while answering the questions? Discuss your group's responses and followup with a few questions—

- If you think you watch too much television, why?
- How could your life be different if television didn't exist?
- How can a young person develop good viewing habits?

4. When the Bible was written there was no such thing as television, so many people think the Bible has nothing to say on the subject. Read each passage and vote as a group about whether or not the verse could be applicable to television.

THE CLOSE

TV is entertainment. Billions of dollars are spend on programming every week. But most of what's on TV isn't real—it's shows offer an escape for those who can't cope with reality. Some youth don't understand that they're watching fiction—shows with beautiful (sometimes perfect) people, numerous special effects, and unrealistic plots.

Brainstorm and make a list of the values that Christians should look for in TV shows. What should Christians keep in mind when watching TV? How do they think saturating their minds with TV shows affects the way they act, talk, and live? How do they think advertisements affect them and what can they do about that as Christians? Challenge them to limit their TV watching and brainstorm other activities they can do to fill the time.

MORE

- What and when are they watching? Ask your kids to keep journals of their weekly TV watching and then bring it in for discussion. Discuss the shows they watched and the amount of time spend watching it compared to the other stuff they did, such as homework, playing sports, eating, talking on the phone, sleeping, and so on.
- And while they're watching the shows, have them pay close attention to the advertisements. What was the ad was telling them? Make a list of all their favorite ads and why the ad appealed to them. Explain that the average 1/2 hour TV show has over 10 minutes of advertisements—how does that affect the way people think about and spend money?

SO, WHAT'S THE DIFFERENCE?

1. What do you think of when you hear the word **hypocrite**?

2. If people tell you they don't attend a church because it is full of hypocrites, what do you say to them?

3. What do you think—**T (true)** or **F (false)**?
   Christians—
   ___ should act differently than non-Christians.
   ___ should talk differently than non-Christians.
   ___ should dress differently than non-Christians.
   ___ should have different priorities than non-Christians.
   ___ are hypocritical to some degree.
   ___ act like Christians if they are truly saved.
   ___ aren't perfect—just forgiven.
   ___ are trying to obtain a perfection that just isn't possible.
   ___ have no special "Christian" behavior.

4. Place an **X** on the scale below, where you see yourself.

   I'm very hypocritical   I'm very Christian-like

5. Which is worse, being a **hypocritical Christian** or **not being a Christian** at all? Why?

6. Read and summarize each passage below in your own words.
   Matthew 6:1-8

   James 1:22-25

SO, WHAT'S THE DIFFERENCE? [h y p o c r i s y]

THIS WEEK

One of the most difficult things for young people to do is correlate their actions to their beliefs. They may express high ideals, yet be unable to carry them out. They rarely notice this trait in themselves, but are quick to point it out in others. This TalkSheet gives you the opportunity to analyze how your youth group and other Christians live up to their Christian beliefs.

OPEN

To start, you may want to try this. Read each of these scenarios and ask the group to decide which one is the most hypocritical. Then make a list of why or why not some are worse than others. What if the people in these situations were Christians? Does that make being a hypocrite worse? What's the difference between lying and being a hypocrite? How do these situations rate on a scale of 1 to 10—ten being extremely hypocritical?

- Stacy is an avid athlete—the star player on the women's basketball team. She excels in taking care of her body, eating right and exercising. Everyone knows that she is a fitness guru. Even though she thinks doing drugs is wrong, she drinks at parties on the weekends—with a few cigarettes once in a while, too.

- Hosea isn't a virgin, but his new girlfriend wants to know what he's done in the past. He doesn't want to bring up the past, so he lies and tells his new girlfriend that he's never had sex. He thinks he's protecting her from getting hurt.

- Hanna goes through money like water. She has exhausted her allowance from her parents and owes at least 20 bucks to each of her friends. But she's been showing up at school with new clothes. Now her parents and friends are wondering what's going on.

- A few of Scott's friends are into Internet pornography and joke about what they see on the web. He's not into that but agrees to go along to a strip club this weekend. After all, he thinks they're two different things.

THE DISCUSSION, BY NUMBERS

1. Ask the kids to share their first thoughts when hearing the word hypocrite. What hypocritical behavior they have encountered?

2. How would your kids respond to this situation? What would they use to defend the church? You may want to role-play the situation and debate each side with your group.

3. How did your kids answer these? What do these questions say about how they see Christians? Take a vote on their responses and discuss each point with the group.

4. To keep this from getting personal, ask your kids where the average Christian teenager may fall on the scale. Why? What about their friends? If you ask some to share where they put themselves, ask for volunteers.

5. What do these passages say about hypocrisy? How did your kids summarize the verses?

THE CLOSE

Close the discussion with a challenge to your group members to practice what they preach. Leave room to talk about God's forgiveness. Also, you may want to discuss tolerance—within reason—for other Christians. God doesn't expect others to be perfect and they shouldn't either.

Communicate that it's easy to fake others out and to pretend to be something they aren't. But God knows their hearts. He knows them better than they know themselves—they'll never fool him.

MORE:

- On a large whiteboard or poster board, draw two columns labeled CHRISTIAN and OTHER. Brainstorm with your youth what characteristics or stereotypes there are of Christians and others. Discuss how Christians are portrayed in the media—on TV shows and movies. How can your kids live in the world without making others feel inferior? How would there lives be different if they weren't Christians?

- What can each of your kids do during the next week to put their faith into practice? Ask them to write their ideas on a 3x5 card (kind of like a pledge) and give them to you. Then, a week or so later, go through the cards and talk about how they did. What was easy or hard about living their faith? What long-term changes can they shoot for?

- God makes it clear that Christians aren't supposed to judge others. Check out and discuss Matthew 7:1-2, Romans 2:1, Romans 14:10, and James 4:11. What do these verses warn about judging?

GOT THE LOOK?

1. If your could change one thing about your **appearance**, it would be—

2. Rank the following reasons to dress in a particular way from **best (1)** to the **worst (10)**.
    ___ I feel comfortable this way.
    ___ I just wear what others expect me to.
    ___ I don't want to be obviously different.
    ___ I want others to notice me.
    ___ I want to please God.
    ___ I wear what I want because I buy my own clothes.
    ___ I dress to please my parents/guardians.
    ___ I dress to show off my body.
    ___ I want to make a good impression.
    ___ I throw on whatever's clean and in my closet.

3. What do you think—**T (true)** or **F (false)**?
    ___ If you look good in it, wear it.
    ___ I'm judged by how attractive I am.
    ___ I usually feel self-conscious about my appearance.
    ___ I dress deliberately to attract attention.
    ___ It's acceptable to follow the latest fashion.
    ___ Most people are hung up on appearance.
    ___ Another's appearance doesn't alter my opinion of them.
    ___ People who are good looking have a big advantage.
    ___ It's okay to have plastic surgery to improve your looks.
    ___ It's worth risking your health to lose weight.

4. How would you rate the following categories? **Matters to God (1), matters little to God (2), matters to God because it matters to me (3),** or **doesn't matter to God (4)?**

    ___ My style of clothing   ___ My physical attractiveness
    ___ My hairstyle   ___ My sex appeal
    ___ My personel hygiene   ___ My overall health
    ___ My height   ___ How much money I spend on
    ___ My use of makeup   my appearance
    ___ My weight

5. Choose one of the following verses, and rewrite in your own words.
    1 Samuel 16:7   Proverbs 31:30
    Psalm 147:10-11

GOT THE LOOK? [physical appearance]

THIS WEEK

Looking good is one of the biggest pressures among youth today—on the TV, radio, from friends, parents, boyfriends or girlfriends, the Internet, and more. It's no wonder than American girls are becoming victims of eating disorders such as bulimia and anorexia. They are a society obsessed with looking good and fitting in. This TalkSheet gives your kids the chance to talk about to physical appearances and discuss how their attitude affects them as Christians.

OPEN

Since the media is the number one influence on our looks, ask each person to cut out at least two pictures from magazines or newspapers that emphasize physical appearance. You can either do this within the group or have them bring pictures from home. What advertisements, articles, pictures, or statistics can they find?

Then take a look at each example and talk about how each one deals with physical appearance. Point out that in most ads, it's the looks of the person that sells the product. What does the picture show? How does that make the reader feel? What is the solution?

You may also want to talk about other media influences that stress good looks, like TV shows or movies. How can your kids keep a healthy perspective of themselves in a culture that idolizes the beautiful people? How can they resist the pressures to look and feel good without going overboard?

THE DISCUSSION, BY NUMBERS

1. Not everybody will want to reveal their answers to this question, but if the kids are comfortable with each other, a few might. Begin by answering it yourself. Why would your kids change what they listed?

2. This will get your kids thinking about why they dress and look the way they do. Most say they don't want to conform, yet their appearance reflects the opposite.

3. Since personal appearance can be hard to talk about, bring up these statements in a general way. Don't ask for personal examples—a few might come out later. And don't be afraid to deal with the hurt, anger, and frustration many of your kids feel about their appearances. Each of your kids will have hang-ups about their looks and that's okay. Remind your kids that they're created by a God who made them unique in their own way. Be particularly sensitive when discussing the issue of harming oneself to lose weight. The number of teenage girls with anorexia or bulimia is alarmingly high, so be careful not to ridicule those who suffer from these disorders.

4. This will bring up a discussion of to what extent God cares about their appearance. Again, keep this discussion general and don't force anyone to share their personal opinions.

5. You may want to divide the group into several small groups and give each one of the a passage to paraphrase and then ask them to share the results.

THE CLOSE

There may be a lot to wrap up with this one! Emphasize that it's okay to want to look good and to take care of our bodies. But your kids shouldn't become obsessed with how they look. God wants us to take care of ourselves, both inside and outside. That means we can look good on the outside, but what's going on inside of us? Are your kids spending time on their character—who they are and what they believe? Are they letting God work in our hearts and minds? How can they balance wanting to look good outside and becoming better people, too?

MORE

● How do people try to change their physical appearance? Brainstorm with your group and make a list of ways that people alter how they look. For example—fad diets, plastic surgery, liposuction, steroids, weight lifting, eating disorders, and so on. How do these change how people feel about themselves? What would God say about spending money and time on these things?

● Some females in your group may be struggling with eating disorders. You may want to spend some time talking about these eating disorders and how to get over them. For information and links, check out the American Anorexia Bulimia Association, Inc. (www.aabainc.org) or The Center for Eating Disorders (www.eating-disorders.com). Be sure to encourage anyone who is struggling with an eating disorder to find help immediately. Emphasize the harm that these disorders cause to relationships, physical health, and emotional health. And be sure to remind them that you are there for them, as is God, who understands the pressures to fit in and look good.

WHAT'S IT ALL ABOUT?

1. In your own words, define **Christian**.

2. What do you think—**R (right)** or **W (wrong)**?
___ If a child's parents are Christian, the child will be a Christian.
___ If a person isn't a Christian, that person will go to hell.
___ There are many good religions—Christianity is just one of them.
___ Once people become Christians, they'll always be Christians.
___ If people doubt God or what the Bible says, they can still be Christians.
___ The main advantage to being a Christian is going to heaven.
___ Christians can disagree with each other about the contents of the Bible.
___ The way people live indicates whether or not they are Christians.
___ Christians don't have as much fun as non-Christians.

3. Put an **arrow** by those that are necessary for a person to be a Christian.

Being baptized   Being born again
Being confirmed   Belonging to a particular church
Accepting Christ as your personal Savior   Reading the Bible and praying every day
Believing the Bible is true   Giving money to the church
Going to church every Sunday   Taking communion
Believing in the virgin birth of Christ   Repenting of sins
Living without sin   Loving God and your neighbor
Looking like a Christian   Believing in Jesus

4. How true are the following statements for you? Rate yourself on each item with a percentage (0% being "None," 100% being "Yup, that's me all the time!")
___ I try to glorify God in all that I do. **(Matthew 6:33)**
___ I strive to follow Christ rather than my own desires. **(Matthew 16:24)**
___ I love the Lord with all my being. **(Matthew 22:37)**
___ I care about and love others as much as myself. **(Matthew 22:39)**
___ I love God and am confident that he has called me to be a Christian. **(Romans 8:28)**
___ I put God and obedience to him first in my life. **(Romans 12:1-2)**

From *High School TalkSheets—Updated!* by David Lynn. Permission to reproduce this page granted only for use in the buyer's own youth group. www.YouthSpecialties.com

59

WHAT'S IT ALL ABOUT? [basic Christianity]

THIS WEEK

This TalkSheet is designed to help explore some of the basic ideas about Christianity. Some of your kids will be on different levels—you may have to add ideas or questions based on your group. You may also want to emphasize specific beliefs or doctrines within the context of this TalkSheet.

Make sure that you do your homework for this discussion. Do the activities on the TalkSheet yourself and look up all the questions you aren't sure about in the Bible. Also, be prepared for those student who won't understand Christian concepts such as born again, be confirmed, or ask Jesus in your heart. Don't assume that your kids will understand all these! You'll probably have to explain a few or all of these.

OPEN

Are your kids listening? How much do they know? Check it out by asking an adult member of your church, a youth sponsor, or your senior pastor to prepare a five-minute message. It should contain some half-truths that aren't biblically correct. These half-truths should be kind of subtle so that they won't be obvious to your kids as they listen. You may want to prep your kids before hand—maybe have them write down any ideas they disagree with. Then see if they picked up any questionable ideas from the sermon.

Or play Bible Trivia—you may be surprised what they do or don't know! You can either pick out some questions before hand or check out www.Biblequizzes.com or www.bible-trivia.com. Split the group up into teams and take turns asking questions.The team with the most points wins the game.

THE DISCUSSION, BY NUMBERS

1. Young people have many varied definitions of what a Christian is. Allow them to share these ideas. If they use words with religious connotations, have them explain what is means—for example, have them give a clear definition of the word saved. You may want to end with a final group definition.

2. These statements are formulated to stimulate discussion about the Christian life, basic doctrines, and particular doctrines related to your church. Don't be afraid to leave a point unresolved or to permit differences of opinion

3. Read this list aloud, asking which items are absolutely necessary in order to be a Christian. You may want to prepare Bible passages ahead of time to support your church's beliefs. Be careful not to end up with a lengthy list of necessary things that could turn Christianity into a legalistic religion.

4. Read the Bible passages with the group and ask them to privately choose their percentage level. For discussion, brainstorm ways that they can improve themselves in each of the areas listed, being as specific as possible.

THE CLOSE

Explain, encourage, and invite! You may have kids who need some one-on-one answers about being a Christian. This is an open door for presenting the gospel and salvation through Jesus. Assure them that no question is stupid—they don't have to understand everything about the Christian faith! The Christian life is a journey—even the great theologians struggle with doctrinal issues. What really matters in light of all the issues and questions? Karl Barth said, "Jesus loves me, this I know, for the Bible tells me so."

Encourage your kids to grow in the Christian faith, to get reading their Bibles and in conversation with God through prayer. As a Christian, they have a gift to give—the message of God's love and salvation. If they want to understand Christianity better, they need to get to know God better. Encourage them and provide them with ways to learn more about the faith. Recommend a devotional or Bible reading program, organize a small group Bible study— you need to jumpstart them and encourage their walk with God.

MORE

- Do your kids know what a creed is? Do they have their own personal creed? Well, have them write a creed—a statement of their personal beliefs. Encourage them to put it in a visible place and read it when they start to doubt their beliefs or have people question what they believe and why.
- It's important for everyone to have spiritual goals. Have each of your youth write a letter stating their spiritual goals and how they want to grow as Christians. Give them envelopes, which they will address to themselves and seal. Mail the letters to them anywhere from six months to a year.
- You may want to have your kids do some research on the Internet for information on Christian doctrines. Possible topics could be sanctification, conversion, grace, justification, or creation. Some of these can be pretty heavy subjects—be sure not to overload them! You may want to make this a group effort and work with each other.

DRINK, DRANK, DRUNK

1. Place an X on the line indicating your opinion of alcohol.

◆ ▮▮▮▮▮▮▮▮▮▮▮▮▮▮▮▮▮▮▮▮▮▮ ◆

Drinking alcohol is a sin and it's wrong.　　　Sometimes it's good, sometimes not.　　　Drink up! There's nothing wrong with it.

2. When do you think it's okay to drink alcohol? **Circle your top three opinions**.

Never
When you're at parties
When you need to unwind
When you're having a nice dinner
When you're taking communion at church
When you're thirsty

When you're with friends
When you're of legal age
When your parents give you permission
Whenever you want—in moderation
When you're at home
When you're depressed

3. What do you think—**Y (yes), N (no)**, or **M (maybe)**?
___ Alcohol is a drug—like marijuana, cocaine, and heroin.
___ There's nothing wrong with drinking, if you don't get drunk.
___ If you don't drink, people will think you're unsociable or not cool.
___ It should be legal for teenagers to drink beer and wine.
___ The church is behind the times in its views on alcohol usage.
___ Teenagers should try alcohol at least once to see what it's like.

4. Jasmine's life seemed to be falling apart. She and her mother have never gotten along well, her father died several years ago, and her stepfather moved out last weekend. Tonight her mom said she had to work late, but Jasmine knows that isn't true—her mom has a new boyfriend. Jasmine is home alone, feeling depressed, and she goes to the cupboard and pulls out a few bottles. A few drinks won't hurt.

   a. Have you ever had a time when you felt this way? When?

   b. What would you do if you were Jasmine?

   c. What could she do besides drinking?

5. Check out one of these passages, and write a paraphrase in your own words.
   Isaiah 5:11-12　　　　　　　　　　Ephesians 5:18
   1 Corinthians 6:12-13

From *High School TalkSheets—Updated!* by David Lynn. Permission to reproduce this page granted only for use in the buyer's own youth group. www.YouthSpecialties.com

61

DRINK, DRANK, DRUNK [a l c o h o l]

THIS WEEK

The influence of alcohol is everywhere. Teenagers see it used, talked about, and glamorized on TV, on the radio, and on the Internet. Kids of all ages are consuming alcohol of all kinds, from wine coolers to hard liquor. This TalkSheet gives you a forum to discuss drinking and what a Christian young person should do about alcohol.

OPEN

Start by asking the group to think of all the beer and liquor slogans that they can remember from TV, the radio, movies, the Internet or wherever. You may want to videotape some of these commercials and play them for the group. Discuss whether or not they pay attention to the commercials and how these commercials portray alcohol. How is it selling the liquor? Are these commercials good, bad, truthful, and so on? You will be amazed at the number of alcoholic beverage commercials that your kids will know. Keep a list on newsprint or whiteboard to refer to later on.

During this discussion, be sure to set the tone for the discussion by listening carefully to the opinions of each of the group members. Although you'll be tempted to state your opinions, wait until later—they'll be more likely listen to you later and respect your thoughts. And remember to encourage them to respect each other's thoughts. This can be a touchy subject, depending on your group, so try extra hard to keep the discussion moving in a positive, yet challenging direction.

THE DISCUSSION, BY NUMBERS

1. Draw the scale shown and record the kids' answers. You will hear several opinions. Allow them to debate the issues.

2. Ask for a show of hands as the group votes on when they think it's permissible to drink alcohol. Allow them time to defend their opinions, then when most people their age drink alcohol. Read the list again and note their answers.

3. You may want to separate the kids into groups based on their answers to the questions and then let them debate the statements. This is a good opportunity for you to listen effectively and find out what your kids believe. Focus attention on the consequences of drinking—what it does to families, friends, parents and individuals both physically and emotionally. You may want to use examples of people you know (without identifying names) and ask the group for anonymous examples, too.

4. This tension-getter explores some of the reasons people drink, such as escapism and stress relief. Can your kids relate to this situation? Why or why not?

5. After sharing these passages, share what the Bible has to say about drinking alcohol. In all probability, your group may wonder if Christ drank wine, why he turned water into wine, and if the verses apply to alcohol.

THE CLOSE

Young people today associate fun with drinking or doing drugs. Partying, among most teenagers, is synonymous with getting wasted. It's important to communicate to your group the dangers of drinking—not just the moral implications. Drinking ruins lives, destroys families, and causes thousands of deaths each year. High school kids are especially vulnerable to the addiction of alcohol and drugs. Some experts say it takes an adult six months to become addicted, but it takes a teenager only six days. And, drinking is extremely dangerous during these growing years. Alcohol can affect brain growth and may cause permanent brain damage.

Saying no to drinking—and any peer pressure—requires self-control. It takes a strong person to stand up for their bodies and minds. Self-control is a fruit of the Holy Spirit—your kids aren't standing alone. Encourage them to ask God for strength and wisdom to say no. Nothing is too hard for God to help them with.

MORE

● Ask your kids bring in examples of how media portrays drinking. Have them bring in clips of TV shows, advertisements, media clips, songs or other examples of how drinking is shown. Discuss with them how they are being bombarded with pressures to drink and the idea that drinking is okay. How does the media portray drinking? Does it ever deal with the consequences or dangers of it?

● You may want to take some time to talk about alcoholism. This is a commonly occurring disease among families—even Christian families—today. Talk about the dangers of alcoholism and how one can tell is someone is an alcoholic. Point out that someone who is drunk has no right to hit or abuse anyone of any age. If any of your kids are facing abusive situations, encourage them to talk with a trusted adult. For more information on alcoholism and other links, visit NIAAA (www.niaaa.nih.gov).

WANTING IT ALL

1. If you had **unlimited money**, what would you go out and buy right now?

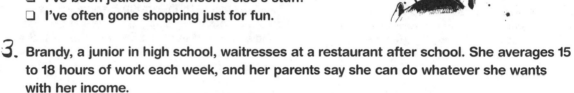

2. Which of the following are true for you?
   - ❑ I've spent money to impress someone.
   - ❑ I've put more food on my plate than I could eat.
   - ❑ I've shopped with my parent's credit card.
   - ❑ I've wished I could have things I couldn't afford.
   - ❑ I've bought something I didn't need.
   - ❑ I've been jealous of someone else's stuff.
   - ❑ I've often gone shopping just for fun.

3. Brandy, a junior in high school, waitresses at a restaurant after school. She averages 15 to 18 hours of work each week, and her parents say she can do whatever she wants with her income.
   What would you do with the money if you were Brandy?

   Do you think her parents are correct?

4. What do you think about these statements? **Y (yes)**, **N (no)**, or **M (maybe)**?
   ___ As Americans, we deserve all we have.
   ___ People have the right to make as much money as they can.
   ___ People in poorer countries deserve some of what we have.
   ___ Money is the root of all evil.
   ___ People should share what they have with others.
   ___ Being rich is a blessing from God.
   ___ It's sinful to spend a lot of money on yourself for things you don't really need.
   ___ It's possible to be materialistic without being rich.
   ___ Teens should be able to work as much as they want.
   ___ It's important to give part of your earnings to the church.

5. Read the following verses. What does each verse say about **materialism**?
   1 Samuel 2:7-8   Matthew 6:19-21
   Psalm 37:7-9   Mark 8:34-36

WANTING IT ALL [m a t e r i a l i s m]

THIS WEEK

Teenagers are saturated in a culture that values money and possessions more than any other. Your kids feel the pressure everywhere they go. Take shopping malls for example—they've become one of America's most popular hang out spots! Teenagers spend more money today than ever on CDs, video games, movies, and clothes. Unfortunately, not much has been done to teach kids about materialism and the dangers of getting caught up in "wanting it all." This session will help your youth understand the materialistic world that they live in.

OPEN

You may want to start by asking your kids to make a list of all the material things that they or their families own. This means everything—beds, TVs, radios, CDs, video games, and so on. Make a list on a whiteboard or poster board. You'll probably end up with an extensive list of items. Some families will have more than one item, like a radio or TV. You may want to illustrate how much stuff Americans have—most of which they don't need to survive! Put a circle around those that are necessary for survival (probably not very many).

Want another idea? Play a version of The Price is Right using pictures of expensive items cut out of magazines. If your group is big, split the group up into teams so everyone can play. Then ask each person or team how much they think an item is worth. Whoever guesses the closest can either (you decide) get a point or gain some amount of money. However you want to play is fine, depending on how much time you have. Whatever team ends up with the most points or the most money wins.

THE DISCUSSION, BY NUMBERS

1. Make a master list of the what your kids want. Have them circle all the things on the wish list that they think they need as opposed to the things they just want.

2. Let your group express their feelings about the difficulty of living in such a materialistic culture. You may want to discuss feelings concerning money and wealth. What do they do with guilt, jealousy, pride, and so on?

3. This situation will bring up a few points for discussion. Should a junior in high school be working 15 to 18 hours a week? Should parents be so lenient? Should Brandy's parents make her buy her own clothes, makeup, and so on? Should Brandy tithe to her church?

4. Ask for a vote on each of the statements, according to the way the kids answered. If everyone agrees on a particular statement, move on to the next. If there are many different opinions, ask them to defend their points of view.

5. Ask some of the kids to read aloud their personalized versions of verses. Then choose one (or more) to discuss in more depth.

THE CLOSE

Materialism is a trap—it's easy to get caught up in wanting it all. Money doesn't buy happiness. The Bible teaches the love of money is idolatry and says "you cannot serve two masters" (Matthew 6:24). Money buys things, but not the things of God—happiness, joy, love, peace—and most importantly, eternal life.

Discuss with the group how Jesus lived and how he challenged his disciples to leave everything and follow him. Although times are different, they're still called to follow him and leave our wants behind. He'll give them what need (and more) if they trust and follow him.

What is one thing that your kids can change about their lifestyle to make them a little less materialistic? Brainstorm with them how to change what they think about possessions. What can they do to make a small change or two?

MORE

- There are many people out there in need of clothes, food, and Christian love. Together with your kids, plan a Christian service project for those who don't have what they need. This can be a big project—possibly traveling to help in another city or foreign country—or something smaller, such as collecting clothing, food, having a garage sale for a charity or working in a shelter.

- Ask several group members find articles or advertisements from magazines or newspapers that deal with spending money, saving money, getting rich, topic like that. Discuss with the group how they are influenced everywhere by the media. What messages does the TV, radio, and Internet send? How are they affected by advertisements see everywhere, from billboards to junk mail?

- How do your kids spend their money? Have them keep track of everything that they spend money on in a given week and write it down. Then talk with them about what they bought and whether or not the item(s) was something they needed or wanted. They'll be surprised to see how they've spent their money!

MUSIC TO MY EYES

1. List **three words** that best describe music videos.

2. How often do you watch music videos?
   - ❏ Every day
   - ❏ Three or four times a week
   - ❏ Once or twice a week
   - ❏ Once in a while
   - ❏ Never

3. How do you decide if a particular music video is **appropriate** or **inappropriate**?

4. Name a popular music video that you've seen and how it would rate on a scale of **1-10** (1 being **totally appropriate** and **10** being **that was the epitome of filth**).

5. How would you respond to the following—**A (always), S (sometimes),** or **N (never)**?
   ___ Music videos don't make much sense to me.
   ___ Teenagers don't take videos as seriously as parents.
   ___ Music videos have nothing to do with the song.
   ___ Music videos exploit women.
   ___ Parents should watch videos to better understand teenagers.
   ___ Music videos are too violent.
   ___ Music videos are fun to watch.
   ___ Watching music videos affects my values.

6. Check out one of the following Bible verses, and summarize it in your own words.
   Galatians 5:13
   Ephesians 5:15-17
   Philippians 4:8
   Colossians 2:8

MUSIC TO MY EYES [music videos]

THIS WEEK

Teenagers today see music videos almost every-where—on TV stations (like VH1, MTV, CMT, etc.), in advertisements, in movies, and on the Internet. There's no doubt that music videos are a huge part of today's visual, interactive culture.

With all these changing factors, it's important to talk about what videos your kids watch, how they are influenced by them, and how they can make decisions about them in the future.

OPEN

You could do several different things to open this discussion—

• Videotape or rent some music videos. Check out TV stations like MTV, VH1 (pop & more), or CMT (country). Be sure to preview the entire tape and all videos before you show them to your group.

• Videotape some commercials from TV that have music videos in them. Most music TV stations will have them, as well as prime time sitcom stations. Show them to your group. Did they like the video ad or not? What did the music video have to do with the advertisement?

• Download some videos from the Internet (www.mp3.com).These usually aren't as clear as the TV, but they show how accessible music videos are on the Internet!

THE DISCUSSION, BY NUMBERS

1. Ask the kids to share their choices. Make a list of their descriptions for all to see, dividing them into two columns—positive and negative.

2. Ask for a show of hands to find out who watches music videos the most and the one who watches the least. Do they watch them on TV, computer CD-ROM, or on the Internet?

3. Discuss their ideas and reach a group consensus. You might want to ask why it's important to be discerning about what they watch.

4. Today's teens have grown up with music videos. Don't assume that they understand why some of the choreography, imagery, or lyrics of some popular videos are wrong or harmful. You may have some explaining to do as various videos are discussed.

It may be helpful for you to watch a video count down show the week of the discussion. These songs will most likely be brought up and your kids will respect your opinions more if you are familiar with what they are watching.

5. Have the kids take a stand corresponding to their votes and share their opinions. Remember to listen carefully to their opinions, without attacking those that may be questionable.

6. You may want to assign the passages to paraphrase and read to the others. How do these verses apply to music videos?

THE CLOSE

Music videos are seen everywhere and are easily accessible. Close by discussing the impact that the music has when your kids can see it and listen to it at the same time.

Your kids must make wise decisions about which videos to watch. Communicate that they have choices about what they put in their minds and bodies. It's important to make the best use of valuable time. Do your kids think watching videos is a good use of time?

Finally, music videos interpret the songs for us—is this good or bad? Does this limit your kids' imagination by controlling their own private interpretation of a song? Do your kids think about a song differently after watching a video? How does it change the meaning for them?

MORE

● There's a fine line between mainstream and Christian bands today. Some Christians bands have crossed over to mainstream (Sixpence None the Richer and Jars of Clay). Some are mainstream bands that write songs that reflect Christian values (sometimes not intentionally) or reference to God. Other bands have Christian members in them, regardless of their music.

Discuss with your kids about what they think classifies a Christian band. What do they think about Christians in mainstream bands? What about those artists that cross over into mainstream music?

Check out *Plugged In* magazine www.family.org/pplace/pi/ (Focus on the Family) or check out www.YouthSpecialties.com for information and links to find discussion topics and latest news on teen culture and Christian music.

● Play a song for your group to listen to. Ask them to write down what they think about the song. What is going on in the song? What do they think the song is about? What pictures can they see in their head? Then show them the video. How does watching the video change their interpretation of the song? How did "seeing" the music change the song?

THE BIG BOOK

1. How would you answer this question? To me the Bible is—
   - ❑ interesting and exciting—my favorite book.
   - ❑ interesting most of the time.
   - ❑ sometimes interesting, but sometimes boring.
   - ❑ boring most of the time and hard to understand.
   - ❑ totally boring and irrelevant—I never read it.

2. What is your **favorite story** from the Bible? Why?

3. Draw a line through the statements that you think are **not** in the Bible.
   - a. God helps those who help themselves.
   - b. The Lord works in mysterious ways, his wonders to perform.
   - c. I can do everything through Christ who gives me strength.
   - d. In all things God works for the good of those who love him.
   - e. Cleanliness is next to godliness.
   - f. Do unto others before they do unto you.
   - g. Do not judge, or you too will be judged.
   - h. All men are created equal.

4. What do you think? Do you A (**agree**) or D (**disagree**)—
   - ___ The Bible is a book of rules.
   - ___ Science hasn't proved the Bible is out of date.
   - ___ The Bible contains contradictions.
   - ___ The Old Testament doesn't apply to today's world.
   - ___ The Bible is a book of mythology.
   - ___ Any translation of the Bible is acceptable.
   - ___ Church tradition is as important as the Bible.
   - ___ The Bible has answers to everyone's problems.
   - ___ The main theme of the Bible is Jesus Christ and salvation.
   - ___ The Bible proves there is a God.
   - ___ The Bible should always be interpreted literally.
   - ___ The Bible is the only book you need to read.

5. What do the following verses say about reading the Bible?

   Psalm 1:1-3   Psalm 119:9-16   John 14:26   James 1:21-24   1 Peter 2:1-3

THE BIG BOOK [the Bible]

THIS WEEK

The Bible hasn't changed over thousands of years. But our youth, our culture, and our world have changed drastically. Sometimes it's hard to apply the Bible to our lives. Some youth don't necessarily believe the Bible is God's Word or has authority over their lives. This session provides the opportunity to discuss the Bible, what today's young people think of it, and how Christians should use the Bible.

OPEN

Give the kids a quiz. Write the names given below on poster board or whiteboard so that they're visible to all. They must decide which books are in the Bible and which aren't, without looking at the Bible's table of contents.

Hezekiah	Matthew	Obadiah
Philippians	Uzziah	Silas
Romans	Nahum	Bartholomew
Acts	Numbers	
Laminations	Judas	
Timothy	Deuteronomy	

Or conduct a short Bible quiz, asking questions about Bible characters to test how much your kids know.

THE DISCUSSION, BY NUMBERS

1. Give the kids the opportunity to share their true feelings about the Bible without making any value judgments yourself. It's normal for young people to think the Bible is boring.

2. Ask the kids to share their favorite Bible stories. What do they think the stories say to them about God?

3. You may want to have them use a concordance or another Bible resource to find these. Statements a, b, e and g are not in the Bible. Statement c is in Philippians 4:13; d is in Romans 8:28; and f is in Matthew 7:1.

4. Ask for a vote on each of the statements, corresponding to the way they answered on the TalkSheet. If there is total agreement on one, go on to the next. If there is a difference of opinion, encourage a debate on their ideas.

5. How do these verses apply to your kids' lives? You may want to choose one or two to discuss further.

THE CLOSE

The Bible is the most sold book in the United States. It's the most sought after book in countries where Bibles aren't available. In fact, it's banned from some countries. The Bible is God's letter to us. He's got loads of important information for us to read and study.

Brainstorm ways that your kids can get into the Bible. Recommend student versions of Bibles including the *Teen Devotional Bible* (Youth Specialties) or the *New Student Bible* (Zondervan). Encourage them to find a version of the Bible that works for them. If an typical NIV is too hard for them to understand, have them find a version that is easier to read.

Challenge them also to read short pieces of scripture at a time. Maybe a few verses or a chapter a day. Have them journal what the verse says to them and how it applies to their lives. See if they can understand how the passage applies to their lives. Sometimes this is hard, sometimes it's easy, but encourage them to stick with it!

You might close by having the kids share their favorite Bible verses with each other. Be sure to share yours and have your other adult leaders do the same. Share why this verse is so special to you and how it applies to your life.

MORE

- Compare different versions of the Bible with your group. This can be interesting and a good way to point out that there's different versions for different people's needs. If you don't have access to different versions, have your kids to some searching on the Internet. There are on-line Bibles available. Assign them verses from different versions and then compare them later on. Discuss why the versions are different. What makes some easier to read than others? Does it still say the same thing?

- You may want to set up an e-mail distribution list with your group and e-mail them a verse every few days. Include a few simple questions for them to think about when they read the verses. Most kids will read their Bibles, but they need encouragement to do it! Also, you may want to start a small group Bible study and discussion with those who are interested. Check out Youth Specialties resources (www.YouthSpecialties.com) for some kickin' materials, including the Creative Bible Lessons series and Downloading the Bible curriculum.

GOD TALK

1. In **three words**, how would you describe your prayer life?

2. If you could pray for **only one thing**—and knew it would be answered—what would it be?

3. How much time do you think Christians should spend in prayer each day? Put an arrow by your choice.
   - A few minutes
   - At least 15 minutes
   - A half hour
   - An hour or more
   - Whatever you can fit into your day

4. What is prayer to you? Read and complete the sentences below.
   - I know God answers my prayers because—
   - I pray because—
   - Praying for me is—

5. Halley knew she shouldn't have gone party with Leon—he had always been trouble. She had lied and told her parents she would be spending the night with her friend Kali. The cops had come to break up the party and now she was panicked—"God, if you get me out of this one, I promise never to go to parties like this again."

   Is it fair of Halley to ask God for help?

   Why should God answer her prayer?

   How would you react, if you were God?

6. Check out one of these verses—and write what it says about prayer.
   Matthew 6:9-19   1 Timothy 2:1-4
   1 Thessalonians 5:16-18   Hebrews 4:14-16

GOD TALK [p r a y e r]

THIS WEEK

Prayer is a conversation with God. Some kids don't think they need to pray or don't feel like it. But both talking and listening to God are crucial for understanding God and growing closer to him. This TalkSheet offers your group the opportunity to take a closer look at the importance of prayer.

OPEN

What is God's model for prayer? Check out the Lord's Prayer with your group. You may want to go through this with your group and break it up into sections. Break your group up into small groups and give each small group a phrase of the Lord's Prayer. Ask them to discuss what the section of prayer means and then write it in their own words. Then together as a group, put all the sections of the prayer together and write a master group interpretation of the Lord's Prayer. Keep this master list for discussion later on and possibly make copies for your kids to take home with them if they need a prayer boost.

THE DISCUSSION, BY NUMBERS

1. What three words did your kids come up with? Why did they chose what they did? What do these words say about the importance of prayer in their lives?

2. Make a master list of what your kids would pray for and why. What if God answered their prayers differently? Remind them that God answers all prayers—go, no, or grow. Go means yes, no means God doesn't want it for us, and grow means wait.

3. How long do your kids think Christians should pray? What are the positives and negatives of spending a long or short time in prayer? Why can some people pray longer than others?

4. Discuss each of these in a general way. You may want to point out that God hears their prayers, loves them, and is concerned about their problems and struggles. Maybe they won't get the result they're are expecting—but it doesn't mean he's not listening.

5. This tension-getter offers an opportunity to discuss prayer in a true-to-life situation. Allow them to debate their views. Prayer isn't designed to be an insurance to get God to help them out of a tough spot.

6. Take some time to discuss these verses. How did the verses apply to their lives?

THE CLOSE

As you close, keep the following points in mind—
- It's hard to have a relationship with God without talking to him—just like it's hard to keep a friendship without talking.
- Prayer isn't magic—it's a conversation with God. He wants us to talk with him, using our own language and letting him know what's on our minds.
- Instead of challenging the kids to do something unrealistic—such as praying for an hour each day—encourage them to begin with two minutes of prayer a day. If they are already praying two, have them strive for four. Challenge them with manageable goals.
- Also, remind them that prayer involves listening, too. Let them know that sometimes it's good to just sit back, relax in a quiet place, and reflect on what's going on in their lives and what God would wants them to do. God doesn't shout out answers, but he does speak to us through our feelings and thoughts.
- Suggest that they keep a prayer journal, or list of prayer requests. This is a great way for them to start their prayers if they don't know what to say. Encourage them to use their letters as a start and write out requests as they go along. This is also a way to look back later and see how God has answered their prayers.

MORE

- With your group, make a prayer request list and encourage them to pray from the list each day. Use this to illustrate the importance of praying for and supporting each other. Encourage your kids to e-mail you with concerns and prayer requests. Then distribute the list weekly to encourage prayer among the group. Include praises in this list, too!
- Encourage your kids to get their thoughts on paper. Challenge them to pray with a pen and paper—to write down things that they are praying for. Have them journal their prayers for a week, then take a look back to see if and how the prayers have been answered. They might have to wait longer than a week. But encourage them to do this. It's a great way to look back and thank God for what he's done!

THIS MEANS WAR!

1. What do you think of when you hear the word **war**?

2. Do you think this statement is **true** or **false**? The world is becoming a more peaceful place.

3. Listed below are possible causes of war. Rank them from **most likely** to cause another war (1) to the **least likely** (11).

___ Terrorism
___ Human sinfulness
___ Greed of leaders
___ Genocide
___ Civil rights
___ Political misunderstandings

___ Poverty
___ Religious differences
___ Overthrow of a government
___ Spread of a country's system of government
___ A mistake

4. What do you think—**agree (A)** or **disagree (D)**?
___ I believe world peace is possible.
___ Our government spends too much money on the military.
___ Christians should not fight in a war.
___ It's a sin to build a nuclear bomb or a biological weapon.
___ War is never God's will.
___ War is necessary because we live in an evil world.
___ Killing someone in war is murder.
___ No one will survive a nuclear war.
___ If we had true faith in God, we would not need nuclear warheads.
___ There will be another world war.
___ Our national defense should be our number one priority.
___ If Jesus was an American, he would serve his country by fighting in a war.
___ There are things we can do to help prevent another world war.

5. Each of these verses says something about war. Check out each passage and write down its main point.
   Isaiah 2:4
   Matthew 24:6-8
   Luke 21:10-11
   James 4:1-2

THIS MEANS WAR! [w a r]

THIS WEEK

Teenagers live in a world full of war and the news of these wars are brought into their homes via television, newspapers, magazines, and the Internet. The threat of nuclear or biological war is a real, persistent threat. This TalkSheet allows you to discuss the subject openly and offers the opportunity to find out how the kids feel about it.

If you or your church takes a strong position on either side of the war and peace issue, you may use this discussion as a way to help your kids understand your view as well as to form one of their own.

OPEN

You may want to start this discussion with a role-play scenario—

Find a political story dealing with war. You can find these on the Internet at any news or history Web pages such as www.cnn.com or www.cfcsc.dnd.ca. Or enter the keywords war or current events in any search engine to find plenty of resources and links.

Read parts of the story to your group to role play the situation. You may want to split the group up into smaller groups for discussion. How will they, as political leaders, decide to act? How will their action affect the world and national relationship? What are the probable consequences?

Based on their beliefs and who is being attacked, each group has five minutes to decide whether or not to take action against this powerful country to stop the violence—knowing that any action will likely start another world war. Discuss their decisions and inform them the focus of the evening will be war.

THE DISCUSSION, BY NUMBERS

1. What do your kids think war is? What are their interpretations of war? What image of war has the media imprinted on them?

2. Does your group think there is peace in the world? Why or why not? What current events are going on that make them question this peace? Take some time to talk about this and how they feel about the current world situation.

3. Ask the group to share their reasons for having war. Do any of these justify war? Why or why not? Decide which reasons are most justifiable.

4. Ask for the reasons for their choices. You may want to have the opposing sides debate their answers. How can they, as individuals, make a difference?

5. Discuss these verses with the group. What do they say about war? How does God view war?

THE CLOSE

Communicate to your youth that war is brutal—it shouldn't be taken lightly. Although war is terrible, it is sometimes inevitable to keep world peace and protect our country. War is the price people pay for freedom and justice. As Christians we should support our country, but strive to be peacemakers. We should fight for and promote peace, acceptance, and love.

Don't leave this discussion in a negative light. Communicate that God is still in control of the world—he knows every person in every corner of the world. They don't have to be afraid.

MORE

● Show a clip of a movie that portrays war. There are quite a few of these—but be sure to preview the clips before you show them. Suggestions include "Saving Private Ryan," "The Hunt for Red October," "Crimson Tide," "In Love and War, " "The Thin Red Line," or "Courage Under Fire." Each of these portray war situations that were before your kids' time! But they still show examples of the pain and human loss involved. Without making this session a history class, quickly debrief on some recent wars and why wars are fought. Why do they have troops in Somalia and in Iraq? Why does our government spend millions of dollars each year to prepare troops for war? How does that make your group feel? What scares them about war situations?

● Have your kids look in the Bible to find passages or stories of war. Share these findings with the group and discuss God's view of war. Emphasize the fact that God allowed the Israelites to fight wars, but at the same time commands us to love everyone. How do they as Christians account for these differences? What does your church say about war and peace?

JUST TRUST ME

1. How would you complete this statement?
Never trust anyone who—

2. Who is someone that you completely trust? What makes this person trustworthy?

   Who is someone that you don't trust? Why not?

3. If you had a friend who lied about you behind your back, what would you do?

4. **Check** the most honest answer for you.

   My parents can trust me—
   - ❏ all of the time.
   - ❏ some of the time.
   - ❏ never.

   My teachers can trust me—
   - ❏ all of the time.
   - ❏ some of the time.
   - ❏ never.

   My friends can trust me—
   - ❏ all of the time.
   - ❏ some of the time.
   - ❏ never.

5. Do you **A (agree)** or **D (disagree)**?
   ___ Overall, the average person can be trusted.
   ___ It's easier to trust Christians than non-Christians.
   ___ I have difficulty trusting people.
   ___ Once a person betrays your trust, it's impossible to trust them completely again.
   ___ It's safer not to trust anyone.

6. **Pick one** of the following verses—what does God say about trust?
   Leviticus 6:2-5
   Psalm 52:8-9
   Proverbs 3:5-6

JUST TRUST ME [t r u s t]

THIS WEEK

Trust is a big issue in the lives of kids today. Some don't trust their parents. Some have been hurt and abused. Others don't have many friends and don't trust other people with their feelings and emotions. It's important to teach them what trust is and what it means for Christians. This TalkSheet will direct your discussion on believing in others and how God fits into this picture.

OPEN

Start by holding an envelope in your hand—with a small prize—either a dollar bill (or more), a gift certificate, or a coupon for a free dessert. Ask your group who would like an envelope. Remind them that they don't know what's in the envelope and that there's a consequence with taking the envelope. Are they willing to risk taking the envelope without knowing what's in it? What makes them trust you or not trust you? Are they going to take the envelope without knowing what the consequences are?

Finally, if someone does take the envelope, ask them in front of the others why they want the envelope and why they trust you. Then hand over the envelope and let them open it. Of course, they won't have to do anything but take the prize!

If no one dares take the envelope, challenge them once more. Then, open the envelope and show them what was inside—a prize. They wouldn't have had to do anything but accept the prize!

This illustrates how trust works. Some people either trust too easily or not enough. Either one of your kids trusted without knowing the risks, or no one trusted at all. Remind them that when they trust a person or something, there are risks involved and consequences that await. Being a Christian involves a risk, too—it means giving your heart and life to God. What are the consequences? Having others look down at you? But what's the prize? They don't have to earn anything. They only have to accept the gift of God's love and eternal life with him in heaven. Not too bad of a free reward, huh?

THE DISCUSSION, BY NUMBERS

1. Let the group share their responses. Some will be humorous and some more serious. You may want to make a list of their responses.

2. Who did your kids chose as trustworthy and not? Why or why not?

3. Most of the kids will have a friend who has betrayed a confidence in some way. Let them share their experiences as long as they don't use names. What have they learned from the experience?

4. This brings the trust issue closer to home. Some kids won't want to reveal their answers, so don't force them. Instead, ask them to think about why others may or may not trust them. What do they need to work on to be trustworthy? Point out that trust is important for all good, healthy relationships.

5. Ask for a show of hands indicating their opinions on these questions. Ask some to share any strong feelings they might have. Discuss how a person can earn trust and how much trust you should extend to a person you don't know very well.

6. Relate these verses to trusting in relationships today. Focus particularly on the fact that we can trust God all them time—he never changes and never will.

THE CLOSE

Communicate that some people simply can't be trusted. Other people seem like they can be trusted, when really they can't. Trust takes time and patience. No one deserves to be instantly trusted. If someone breaks trust, it can take a long time—sometimes years—to be rebuilt.

It's not easy to trust others and for others to trust us—they need to guard our hearts.

They can ask God to heal us when we've been hurt. God forgives us even if people don't. He knows our hearts and can help us become more trustworthy people.

MORE

● On a whiteboard or poster board, write the word TRUST vertically. Split your group up into five smaller groups and give each group one letter of the word trust. Have each group list at least two words or phrases that describe trust and that start with the letter that they've been given. For example, if a group had T, they could list "telling the truth" or "trying to rely on another person". Encourage them to help each other think of descriptions. Then, go over these with the group and discuss what the different phrases or words mean.

● You may want to take some time and talk about what breaks trust. If you sense that some of your kids are struggling with trusting others, they may be dealing with some larger issues, such as sexual abuse, problems at home, or having a hard time at school. Make note of what you see. You may want to have a one-on-one later on with that person. And if you sense an abusive situation, encourage the person to find help—and report it to the authorities in your area.

OH, GOD

1. What is the **first word** that comes to mind when you think about God?

2. If you could ask God **one question**, what would it be?

3. If God wrote you an e-mail about anything, what do you think he'd say to you?

4. Shamir has always felt there was a God, but he's never really felt close to him or felt God really cared about him. Now he's questioning God's existence and has asked you for your opinion. What insight would you share with Shamir for how he can get to know God better?

5. Check one or more of the following statements that **best describes** your relationship with God.
   - ❑ I have a solid relationship with God.
   - ❑ I feel very far away from God.
   - ❑ I want to become closer to God.
   - ❑ God is a mystery to me.
   - ❑ I think that God is pleased with the way I live my life.
   - ❑ I don't have God in my life.
   - ❑ I still have a lot of doubts about God.
   - ❑ A relationship with God scares me. I'm not interested.

6. Check out **Romans 11:33-36**. What do these verses have to say about God?

OH, GOD [G o d]

THIS WEEK

How familiar are you with your kids' beliefs? Do you know about their reasons for believing in God? This discussion will allow you to talk about what your student believe—what they think God is like and how their belief in God makes a difference in their lives. You'll want to make sure that your group members are comfortable with each other before you tackle this discussion. Sometimes it's not easy for them to open up about their beliefs, so be sure to provide a warm environment where they feel supported.

OPEN

You can introduce this in many different ways, depending on the size and maturity of your group. You may want to split them into two groups—one group believing there is a God and one that doesn't. What proof or thoughts to they have that God does or does not exist? How do they defend their answers? What characteristics of God come through during this debate? Keep a master list of their main points for discussion later on.

Or share a story with them about God. Have your kids act out the parable of the lost son (Luke 15:11-27) while you read the story, either from the Bible or another version of the story. How does the parable describe God? What characteristics does God have from the parable? How about the parable of the lost sheep (Luke 15:3-7)?

THE DISCUSSION, BY NUMBERS

1. On the whiteboard or poster board, list all the words suggested. Some people have the wrong picture and may think of him as a cosmic cop, an old bearded man, or a heavenly Santa Claus.

2. Let the kids share their questions and try to answer them as a group. Some simply won't have answers—that's okay. Help them understand that God has answers to our questions, even though they don't always know what they are.

3. Ask several kids to share their e-mails. Did this help them understand God better? What did they learn about God? Emphasize that God has already written us a letter—the Bible. In it, he tells us stories and gives us advice on all kinds of stuff. Challenge your kids to dig in and start getting to know God better.

4. Use this scenario to discuss practical ways to have a better relationship with God. Make a master list of all the suggestions they come up with. You may want to add some of your own. Tell the kids to choose the three they think are the best and to select one of those to do this week.

5. Some maybe will share and some won't—that's okay. What do some teenagers in general think? What questions do your kids have about a relationship with God?

6. These verses list several attributes of God. Make a master list of these qualities. Are there more that aren't in these verses?

THE CLOSE

God thinks so much of all his children. You may want to read a verse or two to the group that describes how much God loves them. Point out that they each are the jewel of God's eye. If he had a computer, their picture would be on the screensaver. He hangs out with them all the time—how often to they hang out with him? If they could chat with God on the phone, what would they say?

Close with a time of prayer. If your group isn't comfortable with praying aloud, then give them some time for silent prayer.

MORE

● It's important to set goals for getting to know God better. Challenge them to do more than just pray and read the Bible—to set specific goals, like praying for ten minutes everyday, reading a chapter from the Bible every other day, or meeting with you and a small group every couple weeks. Encourage them set these realistic goals and write them on a 3x5 card to keep. Remind them that they can come to you with struggles or questions that they may have—everyone needs to be encouraged spiritually.

● Set up an e-mail or snail mail resource for encouraging prayer and scripture. Have your kids e-mail each other or you their favorite verses, new things they've learned, or prayer requests they have. Challenge them to encourage each other to learn more about God. Collect and distribute the e-mails or letters once (or more) a week.

I WONDER

1. **Which of the following do you have doubts about?**
   - ❏ The existence of God
   - ❏ The resurrection of Jesus Christ
   - ❏ The story of Jonah and the whale
   - ❏ The existence of heaven
   - ❏ The truth of the Bible
   - ❏ The love of God
   - ❏ The value of prayer
   - ❏ The virgin birth of Christ
   - ❏ The possibility of miracles
   - ❏ The Genesis account of creation
   - ❏ The reality of hell
   - ❏ The idea that Jesus was and is God

2. **When you have doubts about your faith, which three of the following reactions is typical for you? Circle them.**

   Feel guilty

   Share my doubts with another Christian

   Blame my doubts on the devil

   Ignore them

   Share them with a non-Christian friend

   Get others to doubt the same things

   Assume I'm too ignorant to understand everything

   Talk to God about my doubts

   Ask honest and sincere questions, searching for answers

   Talk to my pastor

   Other—

3. **What do you think? Put an arrow by the one you think is most true.**
   a. Doubts about God are normal.
   b. When I doubt God, he loves me less.
   c. My pastor never has any doubts about God.
   d. God understands and accepts my doubts.
   e. Doubting means a person is losing faith.
   f. If you have no doubts, then you have no faith.
   g. If left alone and unrecognized, doubt will become disbelief.

4. **Turn to Psalm 73 in your Bible, and summarize it in your own words.**

I WONDER [doubt]

THIS WEEK

It is normal and healthy for teenagers to doubt and question what they believe. Most of them are searching to find who they are and what they believe. They're looking for answers and deal with tough questions. It's important for them to be able to discuss these doubts and questions with an adult like yourself. This session isn't able to answer all their questions and doubts, but will help them understand that having doubts is normal, even among adults.

OPEN

Make them wonder! Make a list of the top 10 biggest mysteries or doubts that your kids have—things that your group wonders about. Discuss possible solutions or answers for each one. How will they find the answers, if they can? What baffles them so about these mysteries or doubts? Some of these may include questions about how God made the world from nothing, how Jesus was God and man, if they'll ever travel to Mars, things like that. You never know what doubts or mysteries your kids will have!

Ask your group to role-play situations in which they must defend their beliefs. Split them up into groups and have one group play the devils advocate. One group must defend their side and their beliefs— not only their faith in God, but other issues, like how God created the earth or why there is a heaven and hell. Challenge them to use their Bibles to defend what they are saying. This can be an incredible way to get your kids thinking (depending on your group, of course!)

THE DISCUSSION, BY NUMBERS

1. Ask you group to share what they have doubts about. What statement created the most doubt? What do your kids want to know more about? Be careful not to eliminate their doubts with quick spiritual come-backs. Give them room to discuss these with each other.

2. How do your group members handle doubt? What is the most common answer? Some may not want to share—that's okay. Ask them what the most common reaction of teenagers is.

3. Doubt is almost a prerequisite for developing a strong faith—no faith is required if you are absolutely sure about something. What were their answers? Take some time to talk about concerns that they may have about dealing with doubts.

4. This Psalm deals with doubt. How did your kids summarize it?

THE CLOSE

Tell the story of John the Baptist and how he confidently announced the coming of Christ, then—when he was thrown into prison—began to have doubts about whether Jesus actually was the Son of God (Luke 7:18-19). Doubt is normal—having doubt doesn't mean the loss of faith or that the doubter has sinned.

The Christian writer Frederick Buechner said, "Doubt is the ants in the pants of faith; it keeps it alive and moving." Doubt stimulates closer growth toward God. Challenge them to search for a deeper, more meaningful faith and encourage them to talk to people who trust and care about them. Talking with parents or other responsible, respected adults can strengthen and deepen their faith in Jesus Christ.

Finally, suggest they save their big doubts for God himself, because they may never be answered in this life. We may not have all the answers, but God does. As 1 Corinthians 13:12 says, "Now we see but a poor reflection as in a mirror; then we shall see face to face." God will reveal all truth to us one day in heaven.

MORE

● Several Biblical characters had serious doubts about what God was doing. A few of them were Moses, Abraham, Peter, and Thomas. Ask your group to find examples of doubting characters in the Bible and let them share their findings. Who had doubts? What were the doubts? Are these still concerns that they have today? How did God address the situation? What happened after they understood?

● Challenge your kids to think about trust in light of doubting. What is trust? How does trusting compare to having faith? Do your kids trust only those things that they see? For example, how easy is it to trust God? Would they trust God more if they could see or touch him? How can your kids strengthen their faith in God? How does trusting others affect trust in God? Is it easier to trust people or God?

CAN YOU BUY THAT?

1. Think of your favorite television commercial. What **product** does it advertise?

2. List three **positive things** and three **negative things** about advertising.

3. How do you usually shop?
   - ❑ I don't shop on the Internet
   - ❑ By catalog
   - ❑ Let my mom do it
   - ❑ In outlets
   - ❑ In stores

4. When shopping, do you usually buy **name brand** or **generic**?

5. What do you think—**A (agree)** or **D (disagree)**?
   ___ Advertising uses sex too much to sell products.
   ___ Advertisements are usually ignored.
   ___ Advertising helps people make intelligent decisions about their purchases.
   ___ Advertisements shouldn't feature professional athletes and other celebrities.
   ___ Advertisements generally lie about products.
   ___ Advertising influences people to buy things they don't need or want.
   ___ Advertisers treat consumers as if they were stupid.
   ___ Advertising reaches the subconscious level of the mind.
   ___ Advertisements should never be trusted.
   ___ Advertising should not be done on the Internet.

6. Read the following verses, and write what each one says about **advertising**.
   Ephesians 4:17-19
   Ephesians 5:6
   1 John 3:7-8

CAN YOU BUY THAT? [a d v e r t i s i n g]

THIS WEEK

Our society is engulfed in advertising. Think about it—it's everywhere! It's on TV, radio, billboards, stadium scoreboards, racecars, blimps and airplanes—even on clothing. Companies target younger people to create loyalty to a certain brand. And since teenagers are the age group that spends the most money on CDs, clothes, and moves, they are prime targets. But, they're a bit naïve about what they see and hear. This discussion allows you to point out how false advertising can trick them into the "gotta have it" mentality.

OPEN

Videotape several TV commercials and show them to your group. After each one, stop and talk about the ad. What did the advertisement say? What makes you want (or not to!) buy the product? What is manipulative about the ad, if anything? Explain that companies spend millions of dollars in advertising every year. On a given Super Bowl Sunday, companies spend millions for every second of airtime. Why do they put so much money and energy into advertising? What are some of the best advertisements that your kids have seen? Why did they like them?

Another good lead-in is to make a list of advertising slogans and have the kids guess the product each represents. Or have your kids list slogans for products like make up, perfume or cologne, video games, cereal, soft drinks, shampoo, cars, etc. You'll be amazed what they remember and recognize! Feel free to use this as a game and give points to teams who can name the most slogans in a given amount of time.

THE DISCUSSION, BY NUMBERS

1. Let the kids share their favorite commercials. Why do they like them? Have they bought the product? Why or why not?

2. Make a master list of the responses and refer to them during the rest of the discussion. Why is advertising good or bad? How necessary is it in some cases?

3. Why do they shop where they do? Why do those who shop on-line why they prefer it to actual stores? Do the products meet their expectations when they finally arrive? What are the pros and cons of shopping by the Web, catalog, or in a store?

4. Most will respond by saying, "It depends..." A good way to handle this is to make two lists, one of advertised brands and another brand. Then write the reasons given for each answer.

5. These statements will generate a variety of responses. Allow the kids to debate the different issues that arise with each. You may want divide them up according to their answers.

6. How do these verses apply to advertising? What would God say about the media and how it sells to the public?

THE CLOSE

Challenge your kids to take a close look at the ads they watch and hear. Since the goal is to make money, advertisers will always try to make the product look good. Talk about ways that they can discern these messages. What questions can they ask when they see or hear an ad? How can they limit the amount of ads that they see or hear?

Communicate how God views money and advertising. Getting caught up in the "gotta have it" mentality is unhealthy and sinful. They start to want more and more—soon they become more greedy and unhappy with what they have. God wants us to be content and to rely on him. How does advertising affect the way they view God?

MORE

● Ask your group to keep a list of everywhere they see advertisements. Your kids might not realize just how surrounded they are. Challenge them to take a close look around them during the week as they go to school and hang out with friends. Have them keep an eye out for ads on clothing, on buses, on the Internet, and even on cereal boxes. Have them bring their lists and talk about them. Where did they see advertising? How did it make them feel?

● What impact has advertising had on national holidays, especially Christmas? Talk about advertising in this context. How would they view Christmas if they didn't have to shop, buy, or receive gifts? What if there were no Easter bunnies or gifts from Santa? What if Valentine's Day was just about showing love and not giving away roses, candy, or paper cards? What meaning has the media and society given (both religious and not) our holidays, like Easter or Thanksgiving? Make a two-column list—WITH ADS and WITHOUT ADS. Have them list words or ideas about each holiday from these perspectives.

JESUS GIVEAWAY

1. **True** or **false**? Most of my friends aren't interested in hearing about Jesus Christ.

2. Why do you think most Christian teenagers don't share Christ with their friends?
   - ❏ They feel embarrassed.
   - ❏ They don't think it's important.
   - ❏ They think Christianity isn't fun.
   - ❏ They don't know how.
   - ❏ They're afraid.
   - ❏ They don't want to offend anyone.
   - ❏ They think someone might laugh at them.
   - ❏ Other—

3. Choose **three** effective ways to share Christ with others.
   - ❏ Hand out gospel tracts.
   - ❏ Carry a Bible to school.
   - ❏ Talk to my date about Jesus.
   - ❏ Invite a friend to church.
   - ❏ Live a moral life through example.
   - ❏ Show love to others.
   - ❏ Wear a T-shirt with a Christian message.
   - ❏ Wait for the right opening before talking about Christ.
   - ❏ Bring a friend to a youth group activity.
   - ❏ Give a speech in class about my faith.
   - ❏ Other—

4. What do you think—**Y (yes)** or **N (no)**?
   ___ A true Christian will want to share Christ with someone else.
   ___ A Christian is sharing Christ all the time, even when he or she doesn't realize it.
   ___ In order to share Christ, one needs to have a good understanding of the Bible.
   ___ It'd be better to keep quiet about your faith, than to offend somebody by expressing your beliefs.
   ___ Most people will think you're a freak if you talk about Jesus.

5. Pick one of the following passages to rewrite in your own words.
   Matthew 5:14-16
   Matthew 28:18-20
   Mark 1:17
   Acts 1:8

From *High School TalkSheets—Updated!* by David Lynn. Permission to reproduce this page granted only for use in the buyer's own youth group. www.YouthSpecialties.com

81

JESUS GIVEAWAY [sharing Christ with others]

THIS WEEK

Sometimes it's not easy for teenagers to share their faith with others. It's difficult to explain their beliefs when others are questioning them. Both adults and teens struggle with being a witness, without coming off as radicals. This TalkSheet gives you and your group the opportunity to talk about witnessing and to practice sharing the Christian faith.

OPEN

In this activity, create a role-play situation with you and your group. You may want to get some info in advance to use against your group. Find some facts about other religions and their beliefs. Then present a situation like this—you are a foreign exchange student from India. You grew up in the Hindu religion. Now you're living with an American family that goes to church and worships God. You learned at home that Christians belive in Heaven, not reincarnation. You're confused and feel a bit threatened by these beliefs. You want to know more, but you aren't sure what to ask

Break your kids into groups to brainstorm how they would present the gospel to you, the student. What are they going to say? How are they going to defend their beliefs? Have them write down some points. Then bring the groups together and begin the role-play by confronting them about seeing one of them reading the Bible. Have your kids explain their beliefs to you. Question the kids and get them thinking about their faith and how to defend what they believe.

Afterwards, debrief and encourage them. Explain that it's not easy to explain faith in something that they can't see. If you have suggestions, give them a few things to keep in mind as they witness to others. Then, open the discussion about witnessing.

THE DISCUSSION, BY NUMBERS

1. Many in the group will say the statement is true—their friends aren't interested in hearing about Christ. Ask them to explain their answers.

2. Try to have the group reach a consensus as to which are the top two reasons. What are ways of overcoming each of these obstacles? Are any of these reasons legit? Why or why not?

3. Have the kids share their answers and the reasons why they responded that way. What are the pros and cons of each? Are there other ways that aren't listed? Has anyone ever used one of these ways to reach out? Why are some methods more effective than others?

4. Discuss these statements one at a time. Point out that (1) a true Christian will want to tell others about Christ, (2) we're representing Christ by the way we live, (3) it isn't necessary to know the Bible in order to share Christ, (4) it's a cop-out to think we might be offensive if we share Christ, and (5) we shouldn't be worried about what people think of us when sharing Christ.

5. While talking about these verses, examine the different methods Christ used to talk about himself and how these same methods can be used today to share Christ, such as friendship, helping others, and so on.

THE CLOSE

You don't want to make your kids feel guilty with this session. With their self-esteem on the line, teenagers are reluctant to do or say anything that might embarrass them or cause others to reject them. Be careful not to make witnessing sound like a burden for being a Christian. Emphasize that being a Christian is a gift that each one can give to someone else. How would they feel if they knew a friend could spend eternity in heaven with them? Does this friend know? Brainstorm creative ways they can be witnesses for Christ in non-threatening ways. They don't have to be Bible experts in order to share Christ with others. They can witness in a lot of nonverbal ways through our actions and what they say to others.

Sharing Christ is a privilege—and a command. It's a responsibility that God give us. It's a way to show others that they are loved and that they love others.

MORE

● Missionaries are spreading the gospel worldwide and they need prayer support. Encourage your group to support missionaries, who are witnesses to others worldwide. Challenge them to pray for missionaries, to write them letters, e-mail, and give money. Consider doing a group fundraiser for the missionaries in your church and get the congregation involved, too.

● Brainstorm for a youth group slogan with your group. This could be a logo, statement, or slogan that reflects their faith somehow. Vote on a slogan and a verse. Then—if your kids like the idea—make a kickin' youth group T-shirt. When they wear them, have them keep track of the reactions or questions they get at school. Encourage them to use this as a way to explain their beliefs to others who have questions.

For information on purchasing special order clothing and more, visit the YS links at www.gospelcom.net/ys/central/apparel.html.

SO WHO YOU LOOKIN' AT?

1. On the graph below, where would you rate yourself in **L (looks)**, **S (smarts)**, **PO (popularity)**, and **PE (personality)**. Write the letter(s) of each item on the graph.

At the very bottom   Average   Way on top

2. What are **three things** about yourself that you are proud of?

3. What do you think—**Y (yes)** or **N (no)**?
___ I'm never happy with what I've done.
___ I put myself down a lot.
___ I accept the compliments of others.
___ I feel inferior around people my age.
___ I take criticism well.
___ I think I'm about average.
___ I want to be liked so I do things I shouldn't in order to be accepted.
___ I don't worry about whether or not people like me.
___ I depend on what others say to make me feel important.

4. Roni and Megan have been friends for years. But lately Roni has gotten fed up with Megan—she's been complaining about herself and putting herself down. Roni has noticed that she says things like "I'm so fat" and "I never get asked out!" and mentioned taking diet pills. Roni is concerned about Megan but doesn't know how to confront Megan's behavior.

   How would you confront Megan if you were Roni?

   Why do you think Megan is acting this way?

   How is Megan's behavior hurting her?

   How can Roni be a supportive friend to Megan?

5. Check out the following verses to find out how God sees you.
   Psalm 139:13-18   Psalm 147:10-11
   Luke 16:15   2 Corinthians 5:17-18
   Ephesians 2:10

SO WHO YOU LOOKIN' AT? [self-image and self-esteem]

THIS WEEK

Self-esteem is a huge concern among teenagers. They feel so much pressure to fit in and they worry about their looks, how they act, and if they'll be accepted and liked by their peers. This TalkSheet gives your group the opportunity to discuss self-image and self-esteem and will give you a chance to affirm your kids.

OPEN

Everyone needs to hear affirmations, so have your group give each other a pat on the back—but not literally. Ask each person to trace his or her hand in marker on a piece of 8½ x 11 paper. Then have them tape the papers on each other's backs. Make sure each group member has a pen, pencil, or marker to write with. Then, encourage them to walk around and write something they like about the person in the hand. Although compliments like "I like your shirt" or "cool sneakers" are nice to hear, ask your kids to think of a less superficial comment—maybe something about their personality or talents. Give the group enough time to write on each person's back. Then let the kids read their own papers and share how this activity made them feel.

THE DISCUSSION, BY NUMBERS

1. Don't ask the kids to share their personal answers. Instead, have them think about their answers and what they've learned about themselves. A person's self-image is usually based on how they think others feel about them. Communicate to your kids that they can control how they feel about themselves.

2. Ask the kids to share the traits they are proud of. Or have them share what they would be proud of if they were the person on their right. Keep the focus on personal qualities and accomplishments.

3. Discuss each issue in general terms without asking for their individual answers. You might ask the kids to answer as if they were a typical high school student. They may open up more if you share how you felt about yourself as a teenager.

5. This tension-getter gives you a chance to talk about how to handle others with low self-esteem. What are different ways of handling the situation? How do girls and guys handle these situations differently? What would a guy do if he were Roni?

6. Ask volunteers to read these passages aloud. Do these verses make any difference to them? How do they feel knowing that God loves them unconditionally?

THE CLOSE

Communicate clearly that everyone—even those who look like they have it all together—struggle with self-image. Even parents and adults still feel badly about themselves from time to time. Challenge your kids to begin seeing themselves as God sees them—as his children who he loves. In fact, God commands us to love ourselves as they love others (Leviticus 19:18). It's important to him that they respect and love ourselves as he does!

Emphasize that God has created each of them with potential—and he will use them if they give their lives to him. There are several biblical characters who struggled with self-worth, including Moses (who had a speech impediment) and Paul (who apparently wasn't very handsome and had a "thorn in the flesh"). If they keep putting ourselves down, God can't use us to our fullest and best.

Point out that it is hard to keep a positive self-image when the media tells us otherwise. TV, radio, movies, advertisements tell us how to act, look, dress, what products to use, how be popular, and who to hang out with. They are constantly bombarded with messages that tell us they aren't good enough. But they have control over it—they can keep things in perspective with God's help

God created us in his image. He loves us, cares about us, and died for us. He loves us as they are, not for what they think they should be.

MORE

● What do your kids think about themselves? Ask your kids write a letter to themselves in a self-addressed stamped envelope. Encourage them to write down how they feel about themselves, what they struggle with, and what they'd like to change. Remind them not to be too hard on themselves—no one is perfect. Challenge them to set goals for themselves of what they'd like to work on to improve their self-image. Examples could include not putting themselves down mentally, getting involved in a new group, volunteering their time and building better friendships. Send these letters to your kids after a couple of months. How are they doing? What changes have they made?

● Or check out what the media says about self-image. On a poster board or whiteboard, ask the group to list specific attitudes and messages that the media sends about self-respect and self-esteem. What pressures to your kids feel from the media and others? How do these pressures affect their self-image and that of other teens? How can they resist what TV, radio, the Internet, and movies are telling them?

GO FOR IT!

1. Name **one person** you think is successful, and why.

2. What do you think—
   God wants Christians to be wealthy and successful. **True** or **false**?

3. Answer the following questions by circling your choice.

   a. How important is being popular to you?
   Really important
   Kind of important
   A wee bit important
   Not really important

   b. How important is money to you?
   Really important
   Kind of important
   A wee bit important
   Not really important

   c. Who is the more successful?
   Millionaire
   Professional athlete
   Music legend
   Teacher
   Missionary

   d. What would you rather be?
   Smart
   Powerful
   Rich
   Healthy

   e. What kind of life do you want?
   Exciting
   Spiritual
   Comfortable
   Fulfilling

   f. How do you want others to see you?
   Extraordinary
   Important
   Average
   Special

4. Check out the following Bible verses, and complete the sentences.
   - **Matthew 6:19-21**
     The world says to make as much money as you can, but the Bible says—

   - **Matthew 10:30**
     The world says you're the only person looking out for but the Bible says—

   - **Luke 6:31**
     The world says get as much as you can from others before you are ripped off, but the Bible says—

   - **Luke 16:19-25**
     The world says only beautiful people from the in crowd will it, but the Bible says—

   - **1 John 2:15-17**
     The world says it has a lot to offer you, but the Bible says—

GO FOR IT! [s u c c e s s]

THIS WEEK

Think about it—our society is success-obsessed! They are flooded with different messages about how to look better, make more money, and be more popular. The media tells us that success means having money, prestige, and power. Our youth are convinced that they must have the best clothes, the right friends, and hang with the in-crowd. This TalkSheet will help you talk about the success and what it means for Christians.

OPEN

Your kids may have different ideas about what success is. So in your intro, have them make a list of characteristics of success—what do peers their age need to be successful? In other words, what makes a person successful? Be sure to distinguish between being popular and successful. Use a whiteboard or poster board to keep track of these. Some suggestions may include things like having cool friends, wearing the right clothes, having a boyfriend or girlfriend, and getting good grades. Compare the items on this list and circle the ones are the most important. Discuss which of the items are character traits (being friendly and courteous) and which ones are superficial (such as good looks and nice clothes).

THE DISCUSSION, BY NUMBERS

1. Have the kids share the names they chose. Why did they chose them? Then have them take a vote for the most successful person alive today. How about a person not alive? This will give you a good idea of who your kids consider successful.

2. Ask the group to vote on this true or false statement, debating the issue if there's sufficient disagreement. Help them differentiate between wealth and success, which aren't necessarily the same.

3. These questions get the group thinking about what's important to them. You may want to ask for the answers—or ask what a typical teenager would choose. Let your kids explain why they chose certain answers for c, d, e, and f.

4. Point out there's often a sharp contrast between what the Bible says and what the world says about success. Ask the kids to share their completed sentences.

THE CLOSE

Communicate with your kids that everyone is successful in different ways. Some people do better in school while some others have more friends. God has given people different gifts and abilities that lead to success. But even the most successful people—including very famous, rich celebrities—feel empty and unfulfilled.

The Bible asks, "What does it profit a man if he should gain the whole world and lose his soul?" (Matthew 16:26). Worldly success doesn't last forever. God wants us to seek him and his will first—then he'll bless us with success. Where is your heart? Are you caught up in worldly success or spiritual success?

MORE

● Challenge your kids to ask their parents if they've (the adults) been successful, in their own minds. What do their parents, guardians or teachers think success is? Who do their parents or teachers think are successful people and why? Adults think differently than kids do—they might be surprised who their adult figures think are successful. But help them understand that success doesn't just mean fame. Success is any goal or achievement that one has reached, such as finishing high school, college, getting a job, having a family, and so on. What can your kids do to be successful in their own lives?

● Need a more visual activity? Ask the group to cut pictures out of magazines that portray success according to the media and our society. These may include pictures of actors/actresses, athletes, politicians, or pictures of successful family members or other acquaintances. They may include words that describe or determine success as well. Use this collage to talk about how the media and society views success. What negative messages does it give? What positive messages are there? How does this representation of success compare with that of God's view of success?

YOUTH GROUP SCOOP

1. What's the **best** thing about your youth group?

2. List **three words** that best describe your youth group.

3. If you could change **two things** about this youth group to make it better, what would you change?

4. For each sentence, please write **Y (yes)** or **N (no)**.
___ I'm influenced a great deal by our youth group discussions and activities.
___ I think our youth group has weak leadership.
___ I believe this youth group is Christ-centered.
___ I don't feel like I'm an important part of the group.
___ I attend mostly because my parents make me.
___ I'm doing my part to help make this a better group.
___ I wouldn't be comfortable inviting friends to visit this group.
___ I've grown in my relationship to Christ because of youth group.
___ I give this group high priority in my life.
___ I have a lot of good friends in this group.

5. Check out **Ephesians 4:1-6**, and summarize it in your own words. How can it improve the youth group?

YOUTH GROUP SCOOP [youth group evaluation]

THIS WEEK

Teenagers often take their youth group for granted. When they're having fun and it's going great, they enjoy it. But when there is heavy discussion or less exciting activities, they complain. This session gives you and your group the opportunity to assess the status of the group in a positive way. You can also use this TalkSheet with the leaders of the group as a planning tool.

OPEN

There are a few different ways to approach this topic with your youth group. No matter what, try to stay positive about the group—don't let this turn into a gripe session. Encourage and let your kids talk about other groups they've visited or been part of. Have them share the pros and cons of the activities, leaders, Bible studies, and so on. Jumpstart them with questions like—what did you like about the last group you were a part of? What did you like about the activities? Were you able to talk with the leaders? What made you frustrated? What made you want to go back?

Another intro would be to have your kids list characteristics and features of a perfect youth group. Write the comments down on a poster board or whiteboard so that you can look at them later. Then communicate that no group can be perfect because its members are so different! Each person in the group likes to do different things, which is why it's hard for leaders to please everyone.

Begin by setting the tone and stating that you want to keep the discussion positive. Be sure to note any negative comments that come out, but mediate the discussion.

THE DISCUSSION, BY NUMBERS

1. This is your chance to gauge what your kids like about youth group. You may want to ask more specific questions to get a better feeling for their preferences or activities, bible studies and so on. You may find that your kids have a variety of things they like. Make a note of these for your own reference later.

2. Ask the kids to share the words they chose, and write them on a poster board or whiteboard, in two separate columns marked negative and positive. Why did they choose these words?

3. Let your kids share their criticisms in a constructive way. Remind them the purpose of this TalkSheet is to improve the group, not to bring it down.

4. What would they do differently if they were the leaders? Keep this exercise as positive as possible.

Ask for volunteers to share their responses to the questions one at a time, or to make comments. You may want to ask them to let you collect the sheets at the end of the discussion. Review those later.

5. Ask for volunteers to share what the verse says to them and offer suggestions as how to change the structure of your youth group.

THE CLOSE

If you'd like to do a closing activity, try the affirmation circle. Most teenagers don't hear enough good things about themselves, especially from their peers. It works like this—have everyone sit in a circle with one person in the middle. Those sitting in the circle give compliments to the person in the middle. Don't force them, though—you may have to start them up with a few questions beforehand like—

* What has this person meant to you?
* What does he or she add to the group?
* What are you thankful for about this person?
* Does he or she have personality characteristics that you admire? If so, what?
* Has this person taught you anything about God?

This can be a humbling or possibly embarrasing experience, especially for those who aren't used to hearing compliments. Be sure to include your adult leaders and all your group members.

Finally, let the group know that they are important to the group and that their comments and concerns will be taken seriously. You may want to invite them to get involved in the group activities—possibly help with planning and organizing meetings and events. Then close with a prayer for the youth group and its leaders.

MORE

● Invite your kids who are interested to a planning session to help brainstorm ideas for activities and programs for the coming year. This can be a fun time of reflection and listening to suggestions. Maybe host a special breakfast or dessert night to do this. Encourage them to continue to let you know what they'd like to see happen in the group.

● Have some one-on-one time with your kids who are leaving the group and moving up to senior high. Ask him or her specific questions about what they liked about the year's activities. What new things did you learn? What was their favorite activity? Their favorite discussion? What wouldn't they want to do again? This is a great way to touch base with individual kids and hear their opinions in private.

PROBLEMS PLUS

1. If you could change **one thing** about your life, what would you change?

2. Below is a list of possible teenage problems. Check the three that you think are the most common.

   - ❑ Having no job
   - ❑ Being spiritually down
   - ❑ Being pressured to date
   - ❑ Having health problems
   - ❑ Getting bad grades
   - ❑ Having low self-esteem
   - ❑ Doing drugs
   - ❑ Having no friends
   - ❑ Being bored

   - ❑ Facing their parents' divorce
   - ❑ Being sexually active
   - ❑ Being in trouble with the law
   - ❑ Becoming depressed
   - ❑ Having no car
   - ❑ Having overly strict parents or guardians
   - ❑ Other—

3. What do you think? Circle the answer that best fits you. Compared to most people my age, I have (**more, less,** or **about the same**) problems.

4. Read the statements and decide if they're **T (true)** or **F (false)**.
   ___ Problems are normal and to be expected.
   ___ Most of the problems I have will solve themselves.
   ___ What I do today will determine what happens tomorrow.
   ___ Many times it's useless to try and make things better.
   ___ God cares about every problem I have.
   ___ It's difficult to decide what to do when I have big problems.
   ___ When bad things happen, there's nothing I can do about them.
   ___ Christians have fewer problems than non-Christians.
   ___ I feel far away from God when I'm having problems.
   ___ Talking to someone about my problems isn't easy for me.

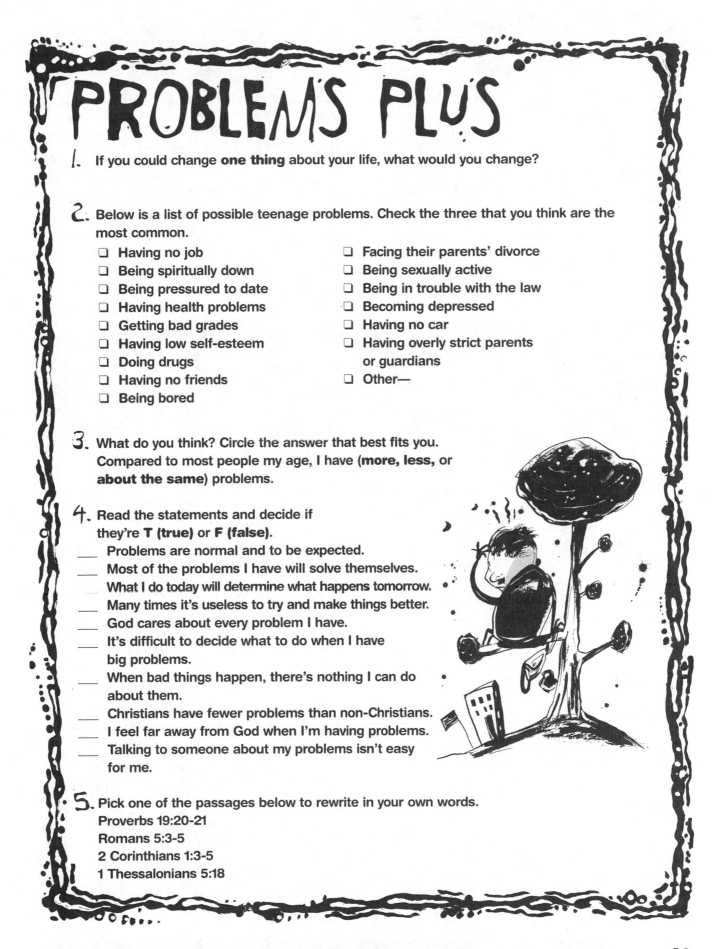

5. Pick one of the passages below to rewrite in your own words.
   Proverbs 19:20-21
   Romans 5:3-5
   2 Corinthians 1:3-5
   1 Thessalonians 5:18

PROBLEMS PLUS [teen problems]

THIS WEEK

Each stage of life presents its own unique set of problems. Most teenagers lack the experience and resources that adults have in dealing with problems. Some teenagers don't know who to go to with certain problems or how to solve them. This TalkSheet will give you an opportunity to talk about common problems, concerns, and frustrations of the high school years, and how to solve them.

OPEN

What problems are high schoolers dealing with? On pieces of paper, have your kids write down problems that they or their peers face. Collect their answers and then read each on aloud. Give the group time to brainstorm ways that each problem could be solved. How do male handle problems different from females? Do teens and adults face problems the same way? Why or why not? How might different people deal with a specific problem?

You may want to list the solutions on a whiteboard or poster board and talk about the different ways to deal with a problem (for example, confronting a person versus talking behind the person's back). Also discuss healthy ways to deal with problems (such as letting your anger cool off versus hitting your brother).

THE DISCUSSION, BY NUMBERS

1. Make a master list of all the changes your kids would like to make. What ones do they have control over and which ones don't they have control over?

2. Ask for a vote on these problems and see which ones are considered the worst. You may want to rate them as a group.

3. How would they answer for teenagers who may be minorities? Disabled? Live in a third world country? Have AIDS or cancer? Your group may soon see their own problems in a different light.

4. Without forcing anyone to share, take some time to talk about each statement and which ones the group chose most often. What questions does the group have about solving problems? What advice do they have for each other?

5. These verses look at problems from different perspectives. Ask for some volunteers to read what their paraphrases of these verses. How do these verses apply to your kids today?

THE CLOSE

Bible characters faced problems of all kinds—one example is the story of David and Goliath. Goliath presented an enormous (and very tall!) problem for David. There were people who probably said to David, "David, look at that giant! He's, well...huge! There's no way on earth that you're gonna win!" But David's attitude as he loaded his sling was "Nope, because the giant is so big, there's no way I can miss!" Communicate with your kids that the biggest problems are chances to grow. That's God's way of making them stronger and more solid in their faith.

Reassure your kids that everyone has problems. As the leader, be careful that you don't gloss over these problems. Be aware that some of your group members may be dealing with some larger, more complicated problems, though—maybe an abusive parent, an eating disorder, or depression. Let your kids know you are available to talk about their problems. If they don't want to or can't talk to a parent, encourage them to find another trustworthy adult like yourself, the pastor, or school counselor. Most important, remind them that God is waiting to listen. Encourage them to take their problems to him. His arms are open wide, waiting to take them in and give them his peace.

MORE

● Have your kids think of the biggest problem that they are facing at the moment. Is it friends? Getting a certain grade in a class? Dealing with peer pressure? Have them write this problem—along with their birthday instead of their name—and explain the problem on the top half of a piece of 8 1/2 x 11 paper. Then pass out the problem papers to some college kids, parents, or other adults for them to write down some thoughts, advice, or favorite verse that would help deal with the problem. Then return these papers to the high schoolers (using their birthdays) and have them respond to the advice that was given. Was it helpful? What kind of advice was given?

Communicate that people who are older have experienced some of the same problems that they do. Use this activity to encourage your youth to seek out adults for advice and encouragement.

● Set up an e-mail (or snail mail) support network for your kids. Encourage them to e-mail you with prayer requests or concerns that they'd like others to pray for. Distribute this list to your group once a week or so. Emphasize the importance of supporting each other through prayer, as well as praying for your own struggles.

WWW.POPMUSIC.COM

1. Now for some info about you!
   My favorite **singer** or **band** is—

   My **favorite song** is—

   My **least favorite performer** is—

   My **least favorite song is**—

2. Circle the average amount of time you spend listening to music every day.

None	1 hour	4 hours
5 minutes	2 hours	8 hours
30 minutes	3 hours	All day

3. Go back and think of your favorite song again. What is it about? Summarize the song's message in one sentence.

4. Read the statements and decide if they are **T (true)** or **F (false)**.

   ___ If a song has questionable lyrics or is performed by someone whose lifestyle is a bad example for others, it isn't good music.

   ___ It's important for Christians to choose music carefully.

   ___ Today's popular music is no worse than music from other times.

   ___ Christians should listen only to Christian music.

   ___ I listen to what I want to, within reason.

   ___ If Jesus were a teenager today, he'd probably listen to the same music I listen to.

   ___ Music really doesn't have that big of an influence.

5. What do you think each passage has to say about listening to mainstream pop music?
   Deuteronomy 6:4-5
   Galatians 2:17-21
   Philippians 1:27
   Colossians 2:6-8

WWW.POPMUSIC.COM [popular music]

THIS WEEK

It's a fact that young people and adults in the church value music differently. Most teenagers listen to different types of music than adults do. And that's okay! Most young people identify with their peer group by listening to the same music as their friends. This TalkSheet was designed to facilitate a balanced discussion in regard to pop music.

OPEN

Begin the discussion by listening to a few different pop music CDs. Ask the kids to bring in their favorite CDs. They like the volume turned up loud, so you may decide to humor them for this discussion, to help you—and them—better understand the music that saturates the youth culture.

If available, bring a few records you enjoyed as a teenager. Most young people are familiar with the music of the all decades, including the 1970s and 1980s.

It is important to introduce this discussion in a positive way, without your youth thinking that you're criticizing their music. Try to be objective and listen to their thoughts and opinions.

THE DISCUSSION, BY NUMBERS

1. Have the kids share their favorites and tell why they chose them. Tally the results on a poster board or whiteboard and find out what performers, songs, and radio stations get the most votes.

2. Find out when your kids listen to music—before school, during lunch, only in the car, only on weekends, and so on. How much time they spend listening?

3. This may show them that many don't even know the message of certain songs. Most people are passive listeners and don't realize what the words are saying! Discuss their favorite songs—do they contain questionable lyrics? What is the message in the song? Does the song talk about moral issues? Point out that although they don't pay attention to the lyrics, the music still gets into their heads and can influence them, even though they don't think it does.

4. Have your kids take turns reading these aloud and find out what they think about each one. Give them time for discussion and hang on to your own comments until the wrap up.

5. Ask a few volunteers to read their applications of these verses to their music. Then discuss why God created music—he wanted us to enjoy it and use it to glorify him. Talk about what kinds of music God would approve of and what he wouldn't like. Point out that he'd want the music they hear to build each other up and encourage us.

THE CLOSE

Pop music is one of many styles of music. No one can keep teenagers from listening to questionable songs and lyrics. Teenagers spend millions of dollars on music CDs every year. It's important encourage them to be aware the kinds of music they listen to and how the music may influence them. It isn't wrong to like pop (or swing, rap, country, or anything else, for that matter), but it's wrong for Christians to spend time and money on anything that doesn't uphold the values of God.

A few suggested questions for them to ask themselves are, "Does this music draw me to or away from God?," "What is this song telling me about my beliefs?," or "Does the song support or oppose Christian values?" Challenge them to pay closer attention to the songs they listen to and to keep these questions in mind.

Now it's time for you to share your values and opinions about music. You may or may not have the same opinion as your kids. Explain what kinds of music you listen to and why. Brainstorm with your group some mainstream and Christian bands that are fun to listen to. Remember that it's not easy to label a band as "Christian"—there is so much crossover today. Encourage them to listen to the lyrics of the songs. What are they filling their heads with?

MORE

- Have the group study the Top 40 list of current hits and rate each song according to the content of the lyrics, the lifestyle of the artist, the music itself, and any other criteria you chose. Rate each one and create your own youth group Top 40 list.
- Encourage your kids to read the lyrics of the songs they listen to. It's surprising how much different a song is after you read the lyrics. You may want to read some lyrics for your kids, discuss them, and then play the song. How did reading the lyrics affect how they understood the song?
- Check out *Plugged In* magazine at www.family.org/pplace/pi/ (Focus on the Family) for the latest trends in music, TV, and movies. This is a useful resource for finding discussion information about news and reviews. Also, check out www.YouthSpecialties.com for information and links to finding discussion topics and latest news on teen culture.

BIG MOUTH

1. Write **three common slang phrases** you or your friends use a lot (keep it clean!) and define them.

2. Share a few of your experiences below.
   A time when you **felt hurt** by something someone said about you.

   A time when you **said something** you wish you never said.

   A time when you **thought something bad** about someone else instead of saying it.

3. In your own words, what does this verse say about your language? "But no man can tame the tongue. It is a restless evil, full of deadly poison." (James 3:8)

4. Which of these scenarios would you consider the **most hurtful** to others? Why?
   - ❑ Reaming out a sibling
   - ❑ Making a snide comment to your mom
   - ❑ Swearing after you stub your toe
   - ❑ Teasing a classmate about their clothes
   - ❑ Telling a teacher that you hate the class
   - ❑ Laughing at someone's mistake
   - ❑ Calling someone a loser
   - ❑ Giving your boyfriend or girlfriend the silent treatment
   - ❑ Cussing out a teammate
   - ❑ Making fun of someone's looks

5. Finish these sentences based on what the verses have to say.

   Proverbs 13:3   It is important to think before I speak, because—

   James 3:5   My mouth can get me into trouble, because—

   2 Timothy 2:16   I want to please God with the words from my mouth, because—

BIG MOUTH [taming the tongue]

THIS WEEK

Teenagers hear harsh gossip, abusive words, and vulgar language everywhere. In fact, most of your kids would consider this normal in society. Certain words are built into our society's vocabulary—it's unavoidable to hear them in movies, on TV, on the radio, in songs, and in our schools. Unfortunately, your kids are able to list words that they hear used everyday—some that are shocking to hear used among middle schoolers. This TalkSheet will help you discuss the relationship between the Christian faith and the words that they speak.

OPEN

Your kids maybe don't realize how much negative language they use. Most of the time it's subconscious—they don't intent to hurt others with our language. Other times they do. No matter what, they've got to monitor the way they speak and the things they say.

Pick a word that is commonly said among your group—not a swear word, just any word that they use a lot. All different youth and groups of kids have slang words or phrases that they use. Pick the word and write it on a whiteboard or a place where the kids can see it. If, during this TalkSheet, someone says the word or words that you chose, have your kids call each other on it. Decide a lighthearted (yet funny) consequence for using this word in the discussion—maybe getting squirt with a water gun or having someone hit a buzzer. Challenge your kids to pay close attention to how they speak and the words they choose. How many times did they call each other on this word? How hard was it for them to keep track of the things they said?

It's hard to monitor our tongue! They use some words without even thinking—including words or language that's crass or mean. This goes for all kinds of swear words, gossip, cut-downs, jokes, and other words that hurt others.

THE DISCUSSION, BY NUMBERS

1. As for your kids to share some slang expressions and explain them. Do they know how the expression got started?

2. Ask the group to share their experiences. Point out how easy it is to get into trouble with what they say. What's worse—saying something bad or thinking it?

3. Words can be deadly and can cause great pain to others. Like physical cuts, hurtful words take time to heal. Our tongue is a weapon—it can hurt others, cause problems, and even destroy relationships. God even warns us about it in the Bible.

4. Decide as a group which one is the worst and why. Who is hurt most in these situations? Which ones can your kids relate to the most?

5. Ask the kids to read their sentences. How do these verses apply to their lives? What can they do as Christians when they are surrounded by negative language? How does loving God affect the way that they treat and speak to others?

THE CLOSE

Blaise Pascal once said, "Cold words freeze people and hot words scorch them, bitter words make them bitter and wrathful words make them wrathful." On the other hand, kind and thoughtful words do wonders. Christians should be generous with them.

Challenge your kids to hold each other and their friends and family members accountable for their language. If your kids struggle with using certain words, have them find a friend or parent that can call them on it. Swearing is like a bad habit—it can be broken. It takes self-control, which other people can help you with. Have them set a personal goal of how they are going to change their language.

Finally, challenge your kids to find one person who they've hurt by their language and apologize for their hurtful words. Communicate how important it is to ask for forgiveness and heal our relationships with others. Take a few minutes to pray with your kids, asking for God's forgiveness and help to control our tongues.

MORE

● How often are swear words really used? Have the group check it out for themselves. Ask each of your kids watch a TV show or movie during the week and keep track of how many times swear words or vulgar language were used. Have them write down the words and how many times they were said. Compare the results the next week. What shows or movies had the most? How did the language fit in with what was going on in the story? What result did the language have, if any?

● Ask your kids to look in their CDs for song lyrics with negative language or swear words and bring them next time. Be careful which ones you read aloud, if you decide to do it. Point out how easy it is to listen to the music and not pay attention to the language. How does listening to music with certain language affect how they think? How does it affect our attitudes and how they treat others?

HUNGER HURTS

1. What is your favorite **food**?

   What is your favorite **soft drink**?

   What is your favorite **dessert**?

2. Why do you eat the **food** you do? Insert an arrow by the most common answer.
   - It's healthy.
   - It's on the menu, and it's cheap.
   - I like it, and it tastes good.
   - It fits into my diet.
   - It looked good on the commercial.
   - It's what my family prepares.
   - It's in the cafeteria.

3. What do you think— **Y (yes, I think so)** or **N (no, I don't think so)**?
   - ___ There fewer hungry people in America than anywhere else.
   - ___ Food is so cheap—everyone can afford it.
   - ___ Powerful world leaders are responsible for starving nations.
   - ___ Fasting and starvation aren't the same thing.
   - ___ Good probably wants some people to suffer hunger.
   - ___ I can relate with people who are starving.
   - ___ The Bible doesn't say anything about fixing world hunger.
   - ___ Starvation occurs after more than a day without food.
   - ___ There's nothing wrong with overeating.
   - ___ World hunger isn't my problem.
   - ___ Starving people have brought it on themselves.

4. In your own words, what does each verse say about hunger and the poor?

   Deuteronomy 14:28-29

   Matthew 25:34-36

   Luke 16:19-26

   Acts 11:28-30

HUNGER HURTS [w o r l d   h u n g e r]

THIS WEEK

Most American teenagers are out of touch with world hunger. They sometimes hear about it, or see pictures of starving people on the news or in magazines, but can't relate with these people. Our society can't expect kids to understand poverty-stricken life. America is a wealthy society that overeats and has the world's highest rate of obesity. This TalkSheet was designed to help your youth think about their own eating habits in light of world hunger and what God has to say about this.

OPEN

You can introduce this a number of ways, depending on your group. If you usually have meetings in the evenings where you serve food—like pizza, soda, chips, cookies or brownies, do something different for this meeting. People in poverty-stricken countries don't have a choice what they get to eat—they don't get yummy treats. In fact they often don't have clean water to drink either. So for this meeting, have whoever makes the food (that might be you) cook up only rice or chicken broth. Serve only one scoop of rice (no sugar or soy sauce on it) or a bowl of broth (without crackers) to each youth. Just one scoop and one cup of water. Explain to them that if they were living in a second or third world country, they wouldn't be complaining about eating rice (or broth) and fresh water. Let them think about that while they're craving steamy, hot cheese pizza! Okay, then later on you can be nice and serve treats—but after the discussion.

Can't go without the pizza? There are posters and descriptive videos available at no or very low cost from organizations such as World Vision (www.wvi.org) or Compassion International (www.ci.org). These give real-life stories and pictures of the poverty and hunger in most second and third world countries. You may want to get one of these and show it to your group as an intro to this discussion.

THE DISCUSSION, BY NUMBERS

1. Who doesn't have a favorite food? You kids will have lots of answers to this one! Without sounding judgmental, point out that in most countries young people have no choice about what they eat. Most people there could never dream of tasting the wonderful variety of foods that they have.

2. After the group has shared their responses, ask them what answers they think hungry youth from starving countries might have given. What if food wasn't a convenience for them?

3. These statements should generate some debate. Let them share their opinions on each one and give reasons why they agree or not.

4. Take a look at theses verses and ask the group how they'd apply them to their lives. They may have some questions like why God allows hunger and why he blesses others.

THE CLOSE

Help the group understand that Christians can't be passive and uncaring about others who have no food to eat. Tony Campolo has said, "Our hearts must be broken by those things which break the heart of God." God loves every starving person in Somalia just as much as he loves us.

Just because they can't go to a starving country doesn't mean they can't help the starving there. Let them know they can actually make a difference. Tell the Bible story about the feeding of the five thousand (Mark 6:38-44) when Jesus used a small lunch to feed a multitude. In the same way, they can support those world relief organizations that God is using to feed the hungry—he will multiply their gift.

It's easy to take food for granted because it's always there. But food is a gift from God. You may want to end the session with a prayer for the hungry people of the world and to thank God for the blessing of food.

MORE

● Organizations like Compassion International, World Vision, and many others rely on financial support. You may want to organize a group fundraising activity for a Christian relief agency. Several ideas include a Saturday afternoon car wash, a pancake breakfast, garage sale, or service auction. Publicize that you are raising money for world hunger and use the opportunity to make others more aware of these issues.

● Challenge your kids to participate in a 24-hour world hunger fast. You can do this as a group in a number of ways. Some groups gather pledges from people and use the fast as a fundraiser. Other groups simply start the fast with a prayer time, fast for 24 hours, and then debrief with a healthy meal at the end. Make sure you do this at a good time of the year when it's healthy for your kids to participate (you don't want parents calling to complain that their child can't play soccer because he hasn't eaten anything!) So, be sure to have parental support and involvement, too.

PG (PARENTAL GUIDANCE)

1. List **three things you like** about your parents or guardians. What are **three frustrating things** about them?

2. Put an **X** on the line scale to indicate where you're moving in the relationship with your parents.

Closer to parents   Way away from my parents

3. If you were one of your parents or guardians—

   What would you do **more**?

   What would you do **less**?

4. What do you think—**T (true)** or **F (false)**?
   My parents or guardians—
   ___ are clueless about my personal problems.
   ___ fight with each other.
   ___ don't trust me.
   ___ don't like my friends.
   ___ won't let me do what my friends do.
   ___ listen fairly to my opinions.
   ___ treat me like an adult.
   ___ try to control too much of my life.
   ___ give me as much money as I want.
   ___ always nag me.
   ___ expect way too much of me.
   ___ don't care what I do or when.

5. Choose one verse, and summarize what it says about parents.
   Deuteronomy 6:5-7
   Psalm 78:5
   Proverbs 1:8-9
   Ephesians 6:1-4

PG (PARENTAL GUIDANCE) [parents]

THIS WEEK

As your youths get older, they'll grow away from their parents and form their own identities. Most of them probably have already! This can cause some stress and rebellion at home. Parents sometimes come off as old-fashioned and too strict. This TalkSheet will help you discuss parent-teen relationships with your kids in a positive way—and hopefully help them see that parents are people, too!

Your kids may come from different types of families, including divorced homes, one-parent families, or foster homes. Be extra sensitive to this as you go through this session. Don't assume that all your kids have traditional two-parent homes.

OPEN

On a large sheet of poster board or on a whiteboard, have your kids write down some things that they'd change about their parents if they could. Jumpstart them if they need ideas—things like "give me more freedom", "don't force me to take piano lessons", and so on. If they don't want to get specific, that's okay.

On a second poster board, have your kids write down some things that their parents would like to change about them—their kids. Keep your kids on track—you might have a kid who writes, "nothing, I'm perfect,"

Now compare the two lists. Point out that both parents and kids have faults and make mistakes—they are all humans! And, point out that parent-child relationships are two-sided—parents and kids will see things differently and that's okay. Remind them that respect is the key issue when dealing with parents. After all, they are being fed, clothed, driven, and paid for by their parents!

THE DISCUSSION, BY NUMBERS

1. Make a master list of positives and negatives of parents or guardians for them to see. What does the group as a whole like the most and least about parents?

2. Where do your kids think the relationships with their parents are going? Some kids don't think it's cool to get along with their parents, others do. Maybe tell them a few things about your relationship with your parents (when you were younger, of course). Once they have shared, brainstorm different ways in which they can improve their relationships with their parents

3. Let your kids share their opinions, but don't let this turn into a gripe session. No parent is perfect. Why did your kids give the answers they listed?

4. Talk about each of these problem areas and watch for the ones where the most frequent response is true. Stop and ask the kids they could change their situation. For instance, how can they earn their parents trust? What are some steps they can take to communicate better with their parents?

5. Ask the kids to read these passages and discuss ways how these verses can be put into practice in their parent-teen relationships. What advice would God have for them?

THE CLOSE

Emphasize that most parents want the best for their kids. They've invested a lot in their kids' lives and care a great deal about them. Parents may not be perfect, but they're the only parents your kids have. God gave our parents to us and we need to be thankful for them.

Encourage your kids to see their parents as people, not just parents. Remind the group that God commands them in Exodus 20:12 to honor and obey their parents, even when they don't feel like it. This command—one of the Ten Commandments—comes with a promise, too. They won't regret loving and honoring our parents.

Finally close with a prayer for everyone's parents and give thanks for them. Give the kids a few moments to pray silently for their relationships and struggles with their parents.

MORE

● Give your kids a parent quiz to do over the next week. To answer the questions, they'll have to talk with their parents to find out the answers. A few good questions to include are—How old were your parents when they first started dating? Where did they go on their first date? What were their majors in college? How did they feel when you were born? How did they celebrate their first anniversary?

● Or invite the parents to your meeting for a broad discussion-type Q & A session. Split up the room with parents on one side and kids on the other. Present some real-life scenarios and have the parents defend their sides to the kids and vice versa. Some situations may include breaking curfew, regulating TV shows and movies, a parent seeing a kid on a questionable Web site, etc. Your parents and kids will have different views among themselves, but it's a great way for your kids to understand their parents more (and vice versa!).

YOU MAKE ME SO MAD

1. List **three things** that make you extremely angry.

2. How would you finish these?
   When my **mom** gets mad, she—

   When my **dad** gets mad, he—

   When **I** get mad, I—

3. What do you think—
   Y (yes, I think so) or **N (nope, I don't think so)?**
   ___ Some people get too violent when they're angry.
   ___ There are positive and negative ways to express anger.
   ___ I have a right to get angry when someone hurts me.
   ___ I get angry often.
   ___ People who lose their tempers are immature.
   ___ Anger really isn't that big of a deal.
   ___ Hiding anger is a good thing to do.
   ___ Anger is a sin.
   ___ Christians should express anger differently from non-Christians.

4. How would you respond to these situations?

   a. Someone swears at you.

   b. Your parents blame you for something you didn't do.

   c. The coach won't put you in the game.

   d. Someone steals your wallet from your locker at school.

   e. A teacher gives you a **D** on your term paper.

   f. You are angry with yourself.

5. Read each verse below and complete the sentences in your own words.
   Proverbs 14:17   When I'm angry, I—
   Proverbs 15:1   When I speak, I—
   Proverbs 29:11   I can control my anger by—
   Ephesians 4:26   If I'm angry I—

From *High School TalkSheets—Updated!* by David Lynn. Permission to reproduce this page granted only for use in the buyer's own youth group. www.YouthSpecialties.com

99

YOU MAKE ME SO MAD [anger]

THIS WEEK

Anger is a powerful emotion and a difficult one to handle, especially for teenagers. It is said that, "Anger, like fire, finally dies out—but not before it leaves a path of destruction." Most young people don't know who to deal with anger. This TalkSheet gives your group a chance talk about anger, healthy solutions, and how a Christian should handle it.

OPEN

Start off by breaking your group up into small groups and giving each group one of the following situations—

• Your parent or guardian grounded you for coming in ten minutes after curfew.
• Your girlfriend or boyfriend lied to you.
• The coach hasn't put you in for five games straight.
• A few of your friends went out last weekend without you.
• Your car stalled on the way to school, and you got a detention for being tardy.
• The teacher loaded you with homework—like you don't have enough to do!
• Your boss always gives you shifts on weekend nights.
• The college of your choice rejected your application.

Ask the small group to brainstorm and make a list of some different reactions to the situation. You can either have them role-play the situations as a group or discuss the different reactions with the whole group. What potential reactions are better—or more effective—than others? How would your kids handle these situations differently? Does anger pay off in these situations? Why or why not?

THE DISCUSSION, BY NUMBERS

1. Make a list of all the things that make your kids angry. How do they usually respond? Why?

2. Have the group share their completed sentences. There are often similarities between how anger is handled by parents and their children. Do your kids react like their parents? Why or why not?

3. Many young people have difficulty expressing anger. They either hold it inside or let it out in destructive ways. Anger is an emotional reaction—not a sin. It's what they do with the anger that counts. Discuss healthy ways to deal with anger—but don't gloss over the fact that it's okay get mad sometimes. Especially if that anger can lead to positive outcomes, like fixing a friendship, mending a relationship, or understanding a situation better.

4. This gives your group the chance to examine appropriate and inappropriate ways to handle anger.

Let them share their responses to the situations. Are some responses better than others? Why?

5. Ask several kids to share their sentences with each other. You may want to point out that Jesus got angry, too (Matthew 21:12-13). Even God gets angry (Joshua 23:16)! Also, point out that God gives us peace and is able to take anger away. Challenge your youth to ask God to help them deal with their anger and ask him to fill them with his peace.

THE CLOSE

Norman Vincent Peale said, "The next time you feel a surge of anger, say to yourself, 'Is this really worth what it's going to do to me and another, emotionally? I will make a fool of myself. I may hurt someone I love, or I might lose a friend.'"

Challenge your group members to deal with their anger in healthy ways. Encourage them to take some time to cool off. Assure them their angry feelings are not sinful—it's the reaction that they need to control.

Also, you may want to discuss what happens when people let their anger go too far. Some of your kids may have abusive parents, broken homes, or substance abusers in their families. It's crucial to communicate that it is never acceptable for a parent, boyfriend, or other person to hit them out of anger. Remind them that if they or a friend is ever in an abusive situation, they must seek help from a trusted adult—a teacher, school counselor, or pastor. Assure them that you are there for them as a confidential source of support and help. For more information and links on physical abuse, check out the National Exchange Club Foundation (www.preventchildabuse.com) or the American Humane Association (www.americanhumane.org).

MORE

● Take some time to talk about the impact of anger in society. List some current situations in the news that relate to anger, such as examples of school violence, gang activity, rape, or other crimes. Communicate that we are a very pressured society—there are so many expectations that people can't deal with. What role can your kids play to be peacemakers among their peers and families?

● Have your kids surf the Internet for information on hate groups—skinheads, neo-Nazis, and white supremacists. You may be surprised at what your kids already know about these groups. Discuss the motives behind these groups, what issues they are angry about, and what your kids can do to deal with these groups.

GOD IN A BOD

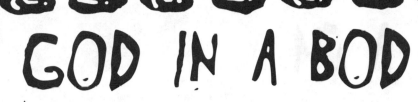

1. List **five words** that describe Jesus Christ.

2. Think about this—if Jesus lived in your town and attended your school, how would you answer these questions?

   - What group of people would he hang out with?

   - What kind of clothes would he wear?

   - What classes would he take?

   - Where would he go to church?

   - What music would he listen to?

   - What would he do after school?

   - What TV shows would he watch?

   - Where would he be on a Friday night?

   - Would your friends like him?

   - What would he be concerned about?

3. If someone asked you why you are a Christian, what would you say?

4. Christ once asked his disciples what others were saying about him (Matthew 16:13). Find out what these verses say about Christ, and complete the sentences.

Matthew 16:16	**Jesus is—**
John 1:1,14	**Jesus is—**
John 3:16-17	**Jesus is—**
John 10:30	**Jesus is—**
Colossians 1:13-23	**Jesus is—**
Hebrews 4:14-15	**Jesus is—**

GOD IN A BOD [Jesus Christ]

THIS WEEK

Who is Jesus Christ? Teenagers need to decide for themselves who Christ is and what they will do with this knowledge. This TalkSheet is designed to focus on Christ and to help them learn more about his character, his attributes, and how they can come to know him personally.

OPEN

On a large sheet of white paper or a whiteboard make a list of words that describe Jesus—his physical looks, his spiritual nature, his personality traits, and stuff like that. Where do they get these ideas? From the Bible? From pictures or models of Christ in church or in stores? What does society say about Jesus? How do they describe him? What do your kids hear about Jesus at school?

How well does your group know the life of Christ? Give the group a list of events in the life of Christ, such as his baptism, the Sermon on the Mount, different miracles, parables. Divide the group teams to compete and arrange the events chronologically. Then, go over the events and explain any story that the kids may not know about or have questions about.

THE DISCUSSION, BY NUMBERS

1. Make a master list of the words the group chose, and let them explain their choices. Which one was most common? Why?

2. What kind of person would Jesus be if he were living today in your town? Put aside the "Jesus in the carpenter shop" image and portray him as a modern-day teenager. This may be challenging—remind them that there's no right or wrong answer. What ideas from Bible verses support their answers, if any?

3. This is a heavy question for some kids, especially those who are new Christians. Don't expect them to open up easily. This may be a good time to share your thoughts about what Jesus means to you. You may want to follow up with a question like, "How does believing in Jesus make a difference in your life?"

4. Check out these verses with the group and then make a summary list of his characteristics.

THE CLOSE

Christ works in each person differently. You may want to share what he has done for you. How has a relationship with him changed your life? John 9:25 says, "One thing I do know. I was blind but now I see!" Explain that your kids can let Christ change their lives—are they willing? Will they let Christ live in them and work in their hearts? The only way to understand Jesus is know him better.

Point out that Jesus is their friend—not an authoritative heavenly being. He is someone who will stay close to them. He understands their situations, needs, desires, temptations, and struggles because he lived on earth as a human. Invite your group to start a personal relationship with Jesus if they haven't already. What will they lose? Nothing. They'll gain the best friend they've ever had.

MORE

- This lesson can't cover everything about Christ. You may want to start a Bible study or small group on the life of Christ. Several materials are available, including *Creative Bible Lessons on the Life of Christ* from Youth Specialties (www.YouthSpecialties.com).

- How is Christ portrayed by the media—on the Internet, in movies, on TV, and so on? Ask your group to do some outside research to find some examples. They'll most likely be able to find both good and bad ones. Discuss the examples they found and how society depicts Christ. Are these accurate examples of Jesus? What do these examples say about Christianity and religion?

- You may want to use this lesson to explain the difference between God and Jesus. Some of your kids may wonder how Jesus can be God if he's God's son. This is tough to explain in simple terms! Be careful not to get too theological, but take the time to explain the Trinity and the relationship between God, Jesus, and the Holy Spirit. Take a look at the TalkSheet Got Spirit? (page 27) for more discussion questions, explanations, and activities.

THE DEVIL MADE ME DO IT

1. **How would you complete these?**

   I'm tempted to do bad things—
   - ❏ more than I used to be.
   - ❏ about the same as I used to be.
   - ❏ less than I used to be.
   - ❏ I don't know.

   Most of the time, when I'm tempted—
   - ❏ I think about it for a while.
   - ❏ I give in right away.
   - ❏ I ignore it.
   - ❏ I ask God for strength.

   When I give into temptation, I usually feel—
   - ❏ guilty or ashamed.
   - ❏ proud or satisfied.
   - ❏ nothing.

2. **Which do you think is the absolute worst? Why?**
   - ❏ Blatantly lying
   - ❏ Cheating on a final
   - ❏ Murdering someone
   - ❏ Stealing from your work
   - ❏ Out-speeding a cop
   - ❏ Chain-smoking
   - ❏ Looking at porno magazines or Web sites
   - ❏ Faking the flu to get out of school
   - ❏ Frequently cursing
   - ❏ Doing drugs
   - ❏ Backstabbing a friend
   - ❏ Plagarizing information off the Internet
   - ❏ Drinking alcohol
   - ❏ Going too far with physical intimacy
   - ❏ Taking a parent's credit card

3. **How would you handle these temptations?**

   If I accidentally logged on to a pornographic Web site, I would—

   If my parents were being unfair to me, I would—

   If I were pressured to have sex, I would—

   If I knew I could get away with cheating on a test, I would—

   If my friends were getting wasted, I would—

   If my friend dared me to shoplift, I would—

4. **If someone asked you how you overcome temptation, what could you say based on these verses?**

   Psalm 119:11
   Luke 22:46
   John 16:33

   1 Corinthians 10:13
   James 4:7

THE DEVIL MADE ME DO IT [temptation]

THIS WEEK

Temptations are everywhere for both teenagers and adults. As your kids get more independence from their parents and approach adulthood, they'll face temptations that they never have before. They'll also realize how temptations can lead to feelings of guilt and failure. Use this TalkSheet to discuss temptation with your group in a supportive, encouraging way.

OPEN

This intro will be sure to get things going. Have your kids write out temptations that they—or teenagers their age—face in their lives (don't have them write names). Then collect the pieces of paper.

Your kids will role-play the temptations that come with each of these situations. Start by asking for three volunteers—one a devil, another an angel, and the third as the a person being tempted (the tempted). Ask the tempted to sit in a chair with the devil on one side, the angel on the other. Pick a situation and read it out loud. Then the angel and devil must work against each other to influence the tempted's decision. You can rotate participants with different situations to get everyone involved.

Afterwards, ask the group how they felt as the person who was being tempted. What was easier to listen to? What pressures were hard to resist? How did they balance their values against what they wanted to do?

THE DISCUSSION, BY NUMBERS

1. When asking for answers, don't force anyone to participate. Point out that teens face temptation now more than they did ever have. Brainstorm ways to resist temptation and discuss God's forgiveness.

2. Which of these would your kids consider to be the worst and why? What do you think makes one sin worse than another? Point that in God's eyes, all sins are equal. How does this make your kids feel? Do they think any of these items aren't sins (like chain-smoking or drinking)? Why or why not?

3. What are some realistic ways for your kids to handle these temptations? Which ones would be easier to get out of than others? Where do your kids go to for strength when facing temptation? Are they leaning on their own strength—or are they asking for God's help, too?

4. You may want to let your kids work on this in groups of two or three. Ask them to write out what they would say, based on these Bible verses. Will these ideas from the Bible help or work for your students? Why or why not? Have a few of them share their responses and talk about these with the group.

THE CLOSE

Temptation is part of being human. Everyone is created by God with a free will—they are responsible for their choices. The choices they make today will affect them in the future. Even though they can make choices, they must be aware of the consequences that may follow.

How can your group members strengthen their faith and resist temptation? What are some ways to protect themselves from Satan's schemes? God gives his followers tools to resist the devil—reading the Bible, memorizing verses, and communicating regularly with God through prayer. The best way to resist temptation is to stay close to Christ—the only man in history who has ever beat the devil on his own turf. You may want to read a few Bible passages to take this further—the temptation of Christ (Matthew 4:1-11) and the armor of God and spiritual warfare (Ephesians 6:10-18).

MORE

● What is one temptation in particular your kids struggle with? Ask the group the following questions to think about—what is this temptation? Are there certain times when they are tempted more than other times? Do certain people tempt them more than others? What can they do to avoid this temptation from now on?

● On a large poster board or whiteboard, have your kids list specific temptations that teenagers face. Some of these include pornography, premarital sex, drinking and drug abuse. Use these examples to set up case scenarios of a girl or guy who is tempted and must chose what to do. Talk about what consequences he or she will face if they give in to the temptation. What may happen if they resist? What if they give in? What impact with this have in a month? A year? Longer? You may want to play devil's advocate to get them thinking.

WHAT, ME WORRY?

1. Put an **X** next to the things that worry you.

   What others think of me
   What grades I get
   How I look
   Who to date
   What job I'll have someday
   How popular I am
   When there'll be another war
   When I'll die
   When my family will have another fight
   How long my parents will
      stay together
   What I'll do beyond high school
   What to do about my problems with
      the police

   When I'll be abused again
   When my parents will get help with
      their addiction
   How I'm doing in my walk with Christ
   How my parents will pay the bills
      this month
   What my drug or alcohol problem is
   doing to my life
   What the world will be like when
      I'm older
   Who I'll marry
   Who my friends are

2. Which answer is **true** for you?
   The more I worry about something—
   ❑ the worse things get.
   ❑ the better things get.
   ❑ I realize it doesn't change a thing.
   ❑ the less it affects me.
   ❑ it gets worse in my mind.

3. How can someone get rid of worry?

4. On the list in question 1, write an **O** next to those items that are **out of your control**. Then write **C** next to the ones that you **can control**.

5. Check out one of these passages, and rewrite in your own words.
   Romans 8:28
   Philippians 4:6-7
   1 Peter 5:7

WHAT, ME WORRY? [w o r r y]

THIS WEEK

Teenagers have way too much to worry about—their looks, relationships, grades, their future, and more. Today's teenager deals with more stress and tension than ever before. This TalkSheet will help your group talk about their worries and insecurities and how their faith can help them through.

OPEN

Start with a worry-version of the game Pictionary. Have your kids write down some random, funny worries that they deal with or think about. Some possibilities include—having body odor, getting a pimple on the nose, flunking a math test, not knowing how to kiss, not knowing your fly is open, not being able to get to sleep, going to the dentist, or passing gas. Collect them and have volunteers from each team take turns drawing these worries. The rest of the group tries to guess what kind of worry is being drawn and the team with the most points wins.

THE DISCUSSION, BY NUMBERS

1. Some of your kids maybe won't want to open up right away, so start them off by talking about some of the things that worried you as a teenager. Use a whiteboard or poster board to write down worries and insecurities that they face at school, home, church, work, etc.

2. Point out that worrying really doesn't help make a situation better. But sometimes worry is okay—it can motivate them to do things that are good. For example, a student who worries about gaining weight starts a workout program. What do your kids think?

3. Brainstorm some different solutions to worrying. List them on a whiteboard for everyone to see. Define the difference between worry—that doesn't change things—and concern—that motivates change. Communicate that worry is a waste of emotional energy that can be better spend solving a problem or finding a solution.

4. Which of these are out of their control? Which ones aren't worth worrying about? How easy is it to give God control over these situations? What steps can they take to make changes or handle worry?

5. After reading these verses, talk about what God thinks about worrying. Explain that worrying is actually taking situations into our own hands and trying to control our lives. Instead of worrying, encourage your kids to give the situations over to God and ask for his peace and guidance.

THE CLOSE

The English word worry comes from a German word, wurgen, meaning "to choke." Worry, in a sense, is mental agony and can weaken the soul.

It's normal and healthy to have worries, but it can be destructive and self-defeating. It's useless to worry about things that they can't control.

Help your kids realize Christians don't have to worry about the past or the future—both are in God's hands. Jesus says repeatedly in Matthew 6:25-34 that they have nothing to worry about. Whether they know it or not, God is taking care of us.

Brainstorm ways that your youth can deal with their worries. Encourage them to talk about their worries with someone else—a friend, a parent, and another respected adult—someone who is willing to listen. Let them know you are available to listen and help.

MORE

- What happens when people get wrapped up in worry? Have your kids list and talk about what worry does to us physically and the outcomes of worry. Address issues like physical stress, anxiety, depression, and what happens when people can't deal with their worries—like suicide and abusing alcohol or drugs. Communicate that worry is more than just a spiritual battle—it's a mental battle, too. What can they do to help themselves deal with their worries?

- Have your youth find examples of things that people their age worry about. They can find examples all over—in teenage magazines, on the Internet, radio, song lyrics, and more. Help them understand that everyone has worries—even famous athletes and celebrities.

- Time for a little Q & A! Ask your group member to write down (anonymously) thing that they worry about. Pick them out and read them aloud. What advice or encouragement do they have for each other? What suggestions to you or other adults have? Where can they go to get more information?

EYES ON THE STARS

1. Who was one of your heroes when you were **young**?

   Who is one of your heroes **now**?

2. Who would you consider to be **most heroic**?
   - ❑ Business tycoon
   - ❑ Music legend
   - ❑ Minister or pastor
   - ❑ Volunteer worker
   - ❑ War veteran
   - ❑ Counselor
   - ❑ Politician
   - ❑ Professional athlete
   - ❑ Sunday school teacher
   - ❑ Television or movie star
   - ❑ Parent
   - ❑ Bible character
   - ❑ Missionary
   - ❑ Author
   - ❑ Teacher
   - ❑ Grandparent

3. **Check three** of the following acts you would consider heroic.
   - ❑ Saving a child from drowning
   - ❑ Telling the truth when it would be easier to lie
   - ❑ Being on the cover of *People* magazine
   - ❑ Getting good grades
   - ❑ Starring in a TV sitcom
   - ❑ Climbing Mount Everest
   - ❑ Volunteering five hours a week at a local food bank
   - ❑ Dating a popular person
   - ❑ Visiting a retirement home monthly to read to the residents
   - ❑ Working on a missions project during vacation
   - ❑ Scoring the winning touchdown in a big game

4. Who is the person you most want to be like when you grow up? Why?

5. Check out these Bible passages. What does each one have to say about **heroes**?

   Joshua 9:9-10   Proverbs 31:10-31
   1 Samuel 17:51   Matthew 4:23-25
   1 Kings 4:29-34

EYES ON THE STARS [h e r o e s]

THIS WEEK

Media has the power to create heroes and heroines. But these celebrities—shaped by TV, sports, movies, or music videos—aren't necessarily heroic. Sometimes their moral behaviors aren't ones that they'd like our kids to follow. This TalkSheet will help you discuss why they look up to certain people and what a hero is.

OPEN

Try this charades-type game! Before your meeting, write names of some heroes and heroines in large letters on individual pieces of 8½ x 11 paper or Post-It notes. You can include different kinds of heroes including (but not limited to)—

- Superheroes—Superman, X-Men, Spiderman, Batman, and so on.
- Sports champions—Tiger Woods, Michael Jordan, Andre Agassi, Brandi Chastain, Marion Jones, and so on.
- Actors—Julia Roberts, Jim Carrey, Robin Williams, Cameron Diaz, and so on.
- Music stars—Madonna, Dave Matthews, Garth Brooks, Faith Hill, Britney Spears, and so on.

Once you've got these on paper, don't let your kids see them. Split your group up into two (or more) teams. Each team will take turns having a volunteer come up to the front. You'll then stick a piece of paper or Post-It on the volunteer's back or forehead (a hat with duct tape on the front works well). Don't let the volunteer see the name of the hero! In a given amount of time (a minute or so), the other group members have to describe the hero or hero-ine on the paper to the volunteer—without saying the name of the person in any context. If the volunteer can guess the name of the hero, the team gets a point.

THE DISCUSSION, BY NUMBERS

1. How many of your kids still have the same hero now as they did when they were younger? Have them share why the person is important to them and considered to be hero-worthy.

2. Try to get a group consensus on this item. Discuss the difference between a hero and a celebrity—heroes do heroic things. They are wor-thy of admiration even if they are not well known. Celebrities are media creations.

3. Point out that heroic deeds don't always bring fame. Fame has nothing to do with morality today—instead it deals with what is popular and trendy. And remind them that a heroic act may be something as insignificant—even helping someone out—if is an act of discipline, obedience, and respect.

4. Ask the kids to share the people they chose. You will most likely get a variety of answers. Take this time to talk about their role models. What traits or characteristics should good role models have?

5. These verses deal with biblical heroes and heroines in the Bible. Discuss with your kids what made each of them heroic and how God used their deeds. You may also want to read Hebrews 11, which discusses heroes and heroines of the Christian faith.

THE CLOSE

Everyone has a hero—but they should be smart about who they choose. The apostle Paul said, "Imitate me." He wasn't boasting! He was saying, "I'll be your hero. You need a hero who acts as Jesus wants him to do. Imitate me as I imitate Christ" (Philippians 3:17, author's paraphrase). Don't model yourself after anyone who does not reflect the values and high standards of the Christian faith.

Challenge your kids to choose their heroes wisely—and also to live heroically through their actions and examples. Some of your kids think they are nobody—encourage them to believe they can do great things for the kingdom of God. Paul wrote (in Philippians 4:13) that "I can do everything through him [Christ] who gives me strength." Let the group members know there are younger Christians looking up to them and talk about ways that they can imitate Christ in their daily lives.

MORE

- Play a group scavenger hunt to find pictures, card-board stand-ups, or magazines with heroic people on them. You may want to split your kids up into groups and give each group a students a list of heroes that they need to "find." They can go to bookstores, shopping malls, grocery stores, or their homes—anywhere where they can find infor-mation or pictures on the heroes listed. Have them either buy or retrieve the information—or just write down the store, place, article, or maga-zine that they got the info from.
- Hold a contest to see who can find the most inter-esting facts about their hero or heroine on the Internet, in magazines, or wherever they can find some information. Whoever brings the most unique, quirky, or interesting fact about their hero gets a prize. Did this info change the way that they feel about their heroes? How?

I AIN'T GOT NOBODY

1. Who is one of your closest friends? List **three reasons** why this person is a good friend.

2. You've been given the chance to order the perfect best friend from e-friends.com! You can chose from the individual specifications below, so that your new friend arrives in ideal form—plus free shipping and handling! As a first-time buyer, you've been given a $25 credit, but each spec will cost you so spend it wisely!

Each costs $6:
- ❏ Money
- ❏ Popularity
- ❏ Intelligence
- ❏ Godliness
- ❏ Compassion

Each costs $5:
- ❏ Good looks
- ❏ Good conversationalist
- ❏ Outgoing personality
- ❏ Sense of humor
- ❏ High moral standards

Each costs $4:
- ❏ A cool car
- ❏ The right clothes
- ❏ Lots of free time
- ❏ Loyalty
- ❏ Dependability

Each costs $3:
- ❏ Common interests
- ❏ Honesty
- ❏ Good listener
- ❏ Generosity

Each costs $2:
- ❏ Nice house
- ❏ Sex appeal
- ❏ Nice parents
- ❏ Same age as you

Each costs $1:
- ❏ Athletic ability
- ❏ Lives close to your house
- ❏ No other friends
- ❏ Very talented

3. What do you think—**Y (yes)** or **N (no)**?
- ___ I choose the right kind of friends.
- ___ I don't like the friends I have now.
- ___ I think a best friend should be a Christian.
- ___ I'm influenced by friends in negative ways more than I influence them in positive ways.
- ___ I get along very well with my friends.
- ___ I have a hard time making friends.
- ___ I think my friends talk about me behind my back.
- ___ I wish I had a best friend.
- ___ I have friends my parents don't approve of.
- ___ I would like to find some new friends.

4. Flip to **Colossians 3:12-14.** What are some characteristics of friendship found in these verses?

I AIN'T GOT NOBODY [friendship]

THIS WEEK

Friendships are the heart and soul of the teenage years. There's hardly anything as important to high school kids than having friends. Everyone wants to be accepted, fit in, and have fun with friends. There's no doubt that your kids will want to talk about friends—how to get them, how to keep them, how to get rid of them, and how to be one. This TalkSheet will help your group discuss friendship from a Christian perspective.

OPEN

If your group is large enough, play the famous friends game. Give everyone a slip of paper with one half of a well-known duo written on it. Among celebrity couples and other well-known duos, some examples include the President and First Lady, Mickey Mouse and Donald Duck, Kermit the Frog and Miss Piggy, and so on. They have to find their partners without saying anything or showing anyone their slips of paper. They'll have to act out their characters in order to find their match.

Or you can play that same game, but with pictures from magazines, newspapers or the Internet. Paste the picture on a piece of paper, then cut the picture in half, so that each kid gets one half of the picture. They must find the person who has the other half of their picture without talking.

Another good intro is to make a long list of qualities in a good friend on the whiteboard, which can include such things as having a lot of money, popularity, intelligence, strong Christianity, kindness, considerate, good looks, sense of humor, same age, has no other friends, lives nearby, good personality, and so forth. Then tell the kids they can choose five qualities for a friend of their own. (Or any number you decide.) Which would be the most important to them? Have a few kids share their choices.

THE DISCUSSION, BY NUMBERS

1. Have the kids talk about their friends and why they are good friends. If they don't want to talk about specific people, have them tell what qualities close friends have.

2. Ask several kids to describe the friend they bought for $25. Concentrate the discussion on which qualities are truly important in a friendship.

3. Discuss these items one by one but don't force anyone to share answers. You may want to focus on friendships that don't meet parental approval. Ask the group why this happens and what they think can be done to remedy such situations. What did they learned from the statements?

4. In this passage, there are eight characteristics of friendship—compassion, kindness, humility, gentleness, patience, forgiving, and loving.
   Emphasize how important it is to think of as qualities that will make them a good friend to others.

THE CLOSE

Read Proverbs 18:24— "A good friend shows himself friendly." In other words, if they want to have good friends, then they need to be a good friend. What does it take to be a good friend? Friendships, like all relationships are two sided—they need mutual respect, consideration, and effort.

Point out that the Bible is filled with stories of friendship—in fact, Jesus himself had many good friends, a close group of men and women with whom he spent a lot of time. He was the perfect example of true friendship—loving, patient, giving. He showed all of us how to relate to others in positive ways.

Jesus also wants to be our friend—he sticks with us through it all. If we have Christ as our friend, we'll be part of a family—a circle of Christian friends. That's what the church (and this youth group) is all about! Close with a prayer, asking God to bless the friendships of your group members.

MORE

● Friendships take work! They need to be nurtured in order to grow. Challenge your kids to nurture their friendships this week. Have them send each of their close friends a postcard or e-mail telling them how much their friendship means to them. Have them go out of their way to encourage their friends and then thank God for the friends he's given them.

● What do your kids need to work on to be better friends to others? Challenge them throughout the week to think of three things that they'd like to work on in their friendships. Do they need more patience? More kindness? Use 1 Corinthians 13:1-13 to guide them. What would your kids like to change about themselves? Have them write these three things down; then list one thing under each that they can do to improve this. For example, if one wanted to be more patient, he or she could write something like, "not grumble when my friend doesn't call me back right away."

● Have the group take a look at the biblical friendships of David and Jonathan (1 Samuel 18 and 19) and Jesus and Lazarus (John 11). What made these friendships good? What qualities of friendship were shown?

RESOURCES FROM YOUTH SPECIALTIES

YOUTH MINISTRY PROGRAMMING

Camps, Retreats, Missions, & Service Ideas (Ideas Library)
Compassionate Kids: Practical Ways to Involve Your Students in Mission and Service
Creative Bible Lessons from the Old Testament
Creative Bible Lessons in 1 & 2 Corinthians
Creative Bible Lessons in John: Encounters with Jesus
Creative Bible Lessons in Romans: Faith on Fire!
Creative Bible Lessons on the Life of Christ
Creative Bible Lessons in Psalms
Creative Junior High Programs from A to Z, Vol. 1 (A-M)
Creative Junior High Programs from A to Z, Vol. 2 (N-Z)
Creative Meetings, Bible Lessons, & Worship Ideas (Ideas Library)
Crowd Breakers & Mixers (Ideas Library)
Downloading the Bible Leader's Guide
Drama, Skits, & Sketches (Ideas Library)
Drama, Skits, & Sketches 2 (Ideas Library)
Dramatic Pauses
Everyday Object Lessons
Games (Ideas Library)
Games 2 (Ideas Library)
Games 3 (Ideas Library)
Good Sex: A Whole-Person Approach to Teenage Sexuality and God
Great Fundraising Ideas for Youth Groups
More Great Fundraising Ideas for Youth Groups
Great Retreats for Youth Groups
Holiday Ideas (Ideas Library)
Hot Illustrations for Youth Talks
More Hot Illustrations for Youth Talks
Still More Hot Illustrations for Youth Talks
Ideas Library on CD-ROM
Incredible Questionnaires for Youth Ministry
Junior High Game Nights
More Junior High Game Nights
Kickstarters: 101 Ingenious Intros to Just about Any Bible Lesson
Live the Life! Student Evangelism Training Kit
Memory Makers
The Next Level Leader's Guide
Play It! Over 150 Great Games for Youth Groups
Roaring Lambs
Special Events (Ideas Library)
Spontaneous Melodramas
Spontaneous Melodramas 2
Student Leadership Training Manual
Student Underground: An Event Curriculum on the Persecuted Church
Super Sketches for Youth Ministry
Talking the Walk
Teaching the Bible Creatively
Videos That Teach
What Would Jesus Do? Youth Leader's Kit
Wild Truth Bible Lessons
Wild Truth Bible Lessons 2
Wild Truth Bible Lessons—Pictures of God
Wild Truth Bible Lessons—Pictures of God 2
Worship Services for Youth Groups

PROFESSIONAL RESOURCES

Administration, Publicity, & Fundraising (Ideas Library)
Dynamic Communicators Workshop
Equipped to Serve: Volunteer Youth Worker Training Course
Help! I'm a Junior High Youth Worker!
Help! I'm a Small-Group Leader!
Help! I'm a Sunday School Teacher!
Help! I'm a Volunteer Youth Worker!
How to Expand Your Youth Ministry
How to Speak to Youth...and Keep Them Awake at the Same Time
Junior High Ministry (Updated & Expanded)
The Ministry of Nurture: A Youth Worker's Guide to Discipling Teenagers
Postmodern Youth Ministry
Purpose-Driven® Youth Ministry
Purpose-Driven® Youth Ministry Training Kit
So That's Why I Keep Doing This! 52 Devotional Stories for Youth Workers
A Youth Ministry Crash Course
Youth Ministry Management Tools
The Youth Worker's Handbook to Family Ministry

ACADEMIC RESOURCES

Four Views of Youth Ministry & the Church
Starting Right: Thinking Theologically About Youth Ministry

DISCUSSION STARTERS

Discussion & Lesson Starters (Ideas Library)
Discussion & Lesson Starters 2 (Ideas Library)
EdgeTV
Get 'Em Talking
Keep 'Em Talking!
Good Sex: A Whole-Person Approach to Teenage Sexuality & God
High School TalkSheets—Updated!
More High School TalkSheets—Updated!
High School TalkSheets Psalms and Proverbs—Updated!
Junior High and Middle School TalkSheets—Updated!
More Junior High and Middle School TalkSheets—Updated!
Junior High and Middle School TalkSheets Psalms and Proverbs—Updated!
Real Kids: Short Cuts
Real Kids: The Real Deal—on Friendship, Loneliness, Racism, & Suicide
Real Kids: The Real Deal—on Sexual Choices, Family Matters, & Loss
Real Kids: The Real Deal—on Stressing Out, Addictive Behavior, Great Comebacks, & Violence
Real Kids: Word on the Street
Unfinished Sentences: 450 Tantalizing Statement-Starters to Get Teenagers Talking & Thinking
What If...? 450 Thought-Provoking Questions to Get Teenagers Talking, Laughing, and Thinking
Would You Rather...? 465 Provocative Questions to Get Teenagers Talking
Have You Ever...? 450 Intriguing Questions Guaranteed to Get Teenagers Talking

ART SOURCE CLIP ART

Stark Raving Clip Art (print)
Youth Group Activities (print)
Clip Art Library Version 2.0 CD-ROM

DIGITAL RESOURCES

Clip Art Library Version 2.0 CD-RPOM
Ideas Library on CD-ROM
Youth Ministry Management Tools

VIDEOS AND VIDEO CURRICULUMS

Dynamic Communicators Workshop
EdgeTV
Equipped to Serve: Volunteer Youth Worker Training Course
The Heart of Youth Ministry: A Morning with Mike Yaconelli
Live the Life! Student Evangelism Training Kit
Purpose-Driven® Youth Ministry Training Kit
Real Kids: Short Cuts
Real Kids: The Real Deal—on Friendship, Loneliness, Racism, & Suicide
Real Kids: The Real Deal—on Sexual Choices, Family Matters, & Loss
Real Kids: The Real Deal—on Stressing Out, Addictive Behavior, Great Comebacks, & Violence
Real Kids: Word on the Street
Student Underground: An Event Curriculum on the Persecuted Church
Understanding Your Teenager Video Curriculum
Youth Ministry Outside the Lines: The Dangerous Wonder of Working with Teenagers

STUDENT RESOURCES

Downloading the Bible: A Rough Guide to the New Testament
Downloading the Bible: A Rough Guide to the Old Testament
Grow For It Journal through the Scriptures
So What Am I Gonna Do With My Life? Journaling Workbook for Students
Spiritual Challenge Journal: The Next Level
Teen Devotional Bible
What (Almost) Nobody Will Tell You about Sex
What Would Jesus Do? Spiritual Challenge Journal
Wild Truth Journal for Junior Highers
Wild Truth Journal—Pictures of God
Wild Truth Journal—Pictures of God 2